Kevin Trudeau's Free Money™

"They" Don't Want You to Know About

Updated: New for 2014

Kevin Trudeau's Free Money™

"They" Don't Want You to Know About

Updated: New for 2014

Kevin Trudeau's Free Money™ "They" Don't Want You to Know About
Updated: New for 2014
Copyright ©2014 by Free Is My Favorite, LLC
All rights reserved.

This edition published by Equity Press
For information, address:

Free Money 2014
PO Box 9198
Pueblo, CO 81008

ISBN 13: 978-0-9819897-4-7

Interior design: The Printed Page, Phoenix, AZ

Manufactured in the United States of America

10 9 8 7 6 5 4 3 2 1
First Version

Contents

Welcome!

I'm back. We're back. Free Money is back.

Well, actually, Free Money has never gone away. I have so much information to share with you that we here at the Free Money offices decided to put out a new, updated version of the Free Money book. We want you to be up to date on all the latest sources of Free Money out there for you—sources that no one else is telling you about. That's what I like to do.

The last book was such a tremendous success, and I will share some of the amazing stories that readers have told us about their experiences finding their Free Money. Life changing stories that are really exciting! And, some big money!

My team has also found some tremendous success stories of people who have found their Free Money using the very methods we talk about in the Free Money books, and they want to share how much money has come to light. We bring you their stories in the hopes they will inspire you to follow their example and start reaping some Free Money of your own.

That's why I write these books. Most of the people who tell me their success stories don't have any special degrees or skills... they are everyday folks. I don't have any kind of degree in finance or any certificates on my wall making me an expert of any kind. I am just a guy who likes to gather information and to share that information with you.

I know that there is Free Money available from government sources—and lots of other places, too. I want you to have the ability to access this Free Money. Someone needs to tell you about it, so it may as well be me. When is the last time your senator, or congressman or representative called you up or sent you a letter telling you that there are ways to get money in these stressful economic times?

I didn't think so.

The government would rather spend its time arguing and pointing the finger of blame and spinning and campaigning and doing who-knows-what than tell you, the people, that there are ways to get some financial aid.

So let me be the one.

Free Money 2014 is updated with the latest up-to-the-minute research, sources and funds. The hard hit economy has everyone needing a little dose of Free Money programs and I want you to know all the time-sensitive information that the government doesn't bother to tell.

As I always say to skeptics, there are no tricks involved. Picking up the phone, or going online, or filling out a form, are tasks any of us can do. The frustrating factor is that the government keeps the lid on this information. The money is there. I want you to know about it and know how to get what is rightfully yours.

If you know my books, you know I always tell you to read the fine print. For this book, the fine print is right here. I don't hide it in the back of the book or in tiny font. The fact is that information and web sites are always changing. Some programs and sites become obsolete. Some new ones pop up. That is why we wanted to give you a current latest edition.

That is also why I tell you that it is possible that some of the data I have included here could possibly become out of date. That's the way of the world with addresses, programs and web site links. As we go to print, we believe we have the latest, most up-to-date info for you. If a web site or foundation is not active when you read this, so be it. Such is life. The point still remains. Free Money sources abound and we want you to get your hands on it. This book will show you how… even if an occasional phone number goes defunct.

The lawyers also tell me that I need to tell you a "disclaimer" and I don't hide it in the fine print. I am not a financial guru and I cannot guarantee that you will receive a hefty sum. I can guarantee that this information is as accurate as possible as we go to print. I can guarantee that many people will get Free Money. I can also guarantee that you will learn some great methods in this book and I venture to guess you will be talking about these Free Money methods for months to come.

Our team has made every effort to ensure that the information printed here is accurate and up to date. If you find something that is out of date, give a holler. If you find more sources not included here, drop us a line. And don't forget: We are always updating you EVERY MONTH with the latest hot new info in the Free Money monthly newsletters. If you haven't signed up for it, do it now!

No matter what your situation, there are tips and techniques included in these pages to land Free Money. If you are having a hard time paying the bills, Free Money is welcome news. Even if you are sitting pretty, Free Money is still Free Money and always welcome.

So many great Free Money stories have come out of the first book that I am confident we will receive just as many success stories, if not more, from this latest edition. I have a hunch you could be one of them.

Are you ready to find out how to find the dough? Let's do it.

Free Money

That is not an oxymoron or a joke. So many people were critics and skeptics when the first Free Money book came out. They thought it was all hype or bulls*#t. And then they tried it. Nothing convinces a Doubting Thomas more than cold hard cash.

The Doubting Thomases, the Doubting Dougs, and the Doubting Debbies landed some Free Money. Doubt turned to belief.

Believe

I've heard it a hundred times. "Kevin, I didn't know what to think of Free Money. It seemed too good to be true. Then I tried it. Some of the ideas you gave worked for me. Some of the ideas you gave worked for my family, friends, neighbors and co-workers. I would not have believed it if I had not received some money. But, now I believe."

> I meet skeptics turned Free Money believers all the time.

We'll get to some of the success stories in a minute, but I want to address all the naysayers and doubters out there. What have you got to lose? Get an envelope and write "Free Money" on it. Do nothing else, and the envelope will stay empty. But give some of these ideas a try, and you might be surprised how fast you fill that "Free Money" envelope.

Let's say you go online and type your name in the database that I will share with you in one of the upcoming chapters, and you discover some Free Money. You will get a check and you will cash it. That money will go in your "Free Money" envelope.

Or you may try another method from another chapter. Or maybe some other idea will trip your trigger. Whatever grabs you; try it. Maybe you'll get some money and it goes in the Free Money envelope.

Get Crazy

I understand the hesitancy. The concept of having money out there that you don't know about may seem a little farfetched. But you'll soon realize that it's not so crazy after all.

Without intentionally setting out to become a "man with a mission," I have become known for blowing the lid off corporate and government behind-closed-doors ways of doing business. There is much the general public does not know, and the fact that Free Money exists is not something freely talked about.

It should be.

I call it like I see it. The fat cats in Washington and their corporate cronies want to control our purse strings. They want a one-way current of cash flow going to them. Sharing the wealth is not business as usual. Not their business mode anyway, but I make it my business.

Feel the Heat

Because I am who I am, famous for exposing corruption, the powers-that-be scrutinize my books. I have become known for my exposés and I catch heat… but I can stand the heat, I am not getting out of the kitchen. I love telling folks that there are ways to get more money into their lives.

I call that being helpful.

Take the Power

If you have read any of my prior books, you know that I am a straight shooter. Whatever information is out there that they don't want you to know about is exactly the information that I want you to know about.

A few years ago, I wrote a book titled *Debt Cures They Don't Want You to Know About.* It sold millions of copies because it revealed all the corrupt and abusive behavior of the people with the power. I blew their dirty dealings wide open and I also revealed probably the most important secret that they don't want you to know about: YOU really are the one with the power!

With this book you hold right now, you will get a whole lot more than knowledge or useful tips. You are capable of getting Free Money! That's power!

Don't Be Bullied

Even though I may get hassled, America is all about free speech. I'm not making up fairy tales about grants or unclaimed assets or other Free Money sources. They are real. They exist.

To me, it is clear-cut. The feds and the banks and the corporations would prefer to keep you in the dark. I prefer to shine the light. In the first Free Money book, I wrote this passage:

It is my curiosity that has launched these information-packed books that have become my life; and truthfully, my curiosity has gotten me into a lot of hot water. Whenever I expose an organization or a group from any business sector or the government, I catch heat. And because I have evolved into the country's leading consumer advocate, I catch a whole lotta heat. And I wouldn't have it any other way.

> I simply want to share the knowledge... share the wealth.

That has not changed.

For me, my business as usual, is to keep telling it like it is. I realize this is a power struggle. I am fighting for the voice to be heard, and they are fighting to squash me. They want me to go away. They don't want you knowing about the dealings that go on with government officials and corporate big wigs. They don't want you knowing that you can claim assets that have been sitting around for years.

I simply want to share the knowledge and in doing so, share the wealth. A little wealth sounds good right now.

Claim Your Power, Claim Your Cash

YOU do have the power. The power comes from knowing what resources are out there for you. I like being a resource guy, a go-to guy, and information guy. I am sort of like an ATM for information.

All of the information I have acquired over the years is available for you to access. I spit it out, and I hope you do something with it. The choice is up to you. I choose to keep learning and keep doing my thing. You have a choice, too. You can claim your power and start to peruse and pursue Free Money sources.

We shouldn't have to "work the system." It should work for us, the hard working, tax paying American citizens. If there is money to be had out there… and it has your name on it… you should know about it and, more importantly, you should have it.

The system may have created hoops for us to jump through, but we can jump. We can jump for Free Money.

Get Your Fair Share

There is nothing wrong with wanting your fair share. You deserve it. Armed with knowledge, you can get it. Knowledge is power. And what you are holding in your hands right now is power. The power to get yourself some FREE MONEY!

In the first Free Money book, I stated that there are billions of dollars available to you in Free Money sources. The fact remains for Free Money 2014: There are still billions of dollars available in Free Money sources.

Since the last book came out, the government has created some new programs and there are more and different ways of finding Free Money. All that is included in these pages. The Free Money has not dried up or dwindled away. Free Money is alive and well; yet still a well-kept secret treasure.

Let me use an example. If your employer cut you a payroll check and it got lost in the mail, it is still your money and it needs to be found and turned over to you. The Free Money premise works on that premise—that there is lost money that has never been turned over to you. It needs to find its way back to you.

The other premise is that there are sources of Free Money out there from the government and private foundations, etc., that you can tap into… programs, projects, grants, credits, rebates, and on and on. The existence of these sources and how to acquire them are part of the Free Money game, too.

Play the Game

In the research that was done for the Debt Cures books, I became aware of so many sources for Free Money. That is how this all began.

Learning ways to cure your debt led to the discovery of Free Money programs. It was enough information to launch its own book, and now there is enough information for another book.

It is not exactly a game, but you can treat it like one. If the government wants to try to play hide and seek with your money, you can play along.

> **All it took was applying some of the methods that are available to ANYONE.**

The information provided here is not just pie in the sky. These are real sources, and real people got real money. These methods work. Many people assume that there is a "catch." They think that they have to fit into a special category in order to qualify for Free Money. They think they have to be at poverty level to get Free Money. They think they have to be—fill in your blank here—to get Free Money.

Many people, you included, might be thinking, "Oh, it sounds great, but it won't apply to me." Think again. I am a mid-aged Caucasian male with a healthy income and I found some Free Money. Can I make it more clear: Do you have to be "low income" to qualify? Nope. Do you have to be a minority to qualify? Nope. Do you have to be a student to qualify? Nope. Do you have to be a senior citizen to qualify? Nope. Do you have to be a farmer to qualify? Nope.

Certainly, there are grants and programs for all of those groups, but I do not fit in any of those categories and I GOT FREE MONEY!

Do It Now

There has never been a better time for folks to get excited about Free Money. When we wrote the first Free Money book a couple of years ago, it was fueled by the amazing amount of Free Money sources we had discovered. It was fueled by the tremendous need of so many people hurting in this downturned economy.

The fact remains the same as what I wrote in 2009:

It is mind blowing. There is money just waiting to be collected. MILLIONS of people qualify! All of the categories that I mentioned above certainly have the opportunity for Free Money (low income, minorities, students, senior citizens, farmers) and any other category that you can think of as well.

Are you a woman? Ch-ching! Are you a small business owner? Ch-ching! Are you an average, hardworking go-to-work-every-day-to-pay-the-bills kind of person? Guess what? Ch-ching for you too!

That's where this book comes in.

I want you to be able to find Free Money. You don't need to wear yourself out searching the Internet, and you don't need to wear yourself out flipping through the material you might find at the library or the bookstore. You just need a one-stop, go-to shop like this book. Right here at your fingertips are pages and pages and hours and hours of research and information.

Keeping It Simple

I like to keep it simple for you. No one has time in their crazy hectic lives to sift through volumes and volumes of fine print. We have done that for you. For me personally, those big fat books with the paper thin phonebook-like pages and listing, after listing, after listing were not helpful to me.

There are government grants available. But instead of me listing them all here and giving you a book that would make a great door stop, I tell you where to look for the grants and how to find the grants that actually work for you. Each chapter provides a way to land some Free Money. There are many other ways to Free Money besides government grants. That is just one source. There are many more.

Maybe you have money in a long forgotten bank account. We'll tell you how to find it. Maybe you have United States saving bonds that you can cash in for cold hard cash. We'll tell you how to do that. Maybe you have tax money due you. We'll tell you how to go about finding that.

> Many of these methods are absolutely simple, quick, and easy.

Laying it out simply works for me. Believe me, if I can do it, you can, too. These methods are simple, quick and easy. Some people find that shocking and that's what makes it more fun.

Grab Your Share of the Billions

It is not a joke or an attention-getting trick to use the word BILLIONS. It is a fact that our government has BILLIONS OF DOLLARS in grants at our disposal. They don't share the knowledge, but they have to share the wealth.

If you qualify for a grant, you are entitled to that money. Grants are an exciting source of Free Money. Getting cash from the government you do not have to pay back has an extra sense of thrill about it. Sure, I could find a twenty-dollar bill in an old coat pocket and that would make me happy, but getting a free twenty-dollar bill from Uncle Sam just has a little more excitement to it.

The billions of dollars in government grants are detailed in this book for you. We tell you what to do, how to do it and where to do it. Finding them is not as tricky as you may think. Fill out a form; maybe a couple of pages and Free Money could be on its way to you. I will break down how to do it.

Chapter by chapter, step by step. Free Money. Free Money. Free Money.

Free Money is great. Free stuff is great. And, free services are great, too. Maybe you are interested in free legal services. We have a chapter on that. How about free dental, medical or prescriptions? We have that in here. How to get Free Money out of your house? We talk about that, too.

The format will stay similar to the first book so you can easily flip through and see the topics and how you can walk through and be on your way to Free Money.

Enjoy the Feast

Things have been skimpy these last few years. The recession or the depression or whatever you want to call it still drags on. Unemployment numbers are high. People are getting foreclosed and losing their homes in record numbers. Bankruptcies are common and frequent.

The economy certainly does not feel like a feast. And we are hungry.

Let me share what I wrote in the first book. I hope it makes your mouth start to water in anticipation:

I imagine a big buffet table. There are several silver covered dishes. All you have to do is lift the lid to see what is in there. Each chapter is kind of like that… an item at the buffet table. Maybe it appeals to you; maybe it does not. But if it does, by all means, sample. This buffet is all you can take.

If you subscribe to magazines, many include a recipe or two. All of those recipes are tested before they print them in the magazine for you. They try the recipe to make sure it works and make sure the food tastes good. We sort of did that with Free Money in a sense.

As I mentioned earlier, when we did the first Free Money book, we did some of our own research. I quickly and easily did one method and ch-ching, a couple hundred bucks for Kevin Trudeau. Very cool.

Did I stop there? Of course not! This is an all-you-can-eat buffet.

I tried something else. Ch-ching. Another $1,500 for me.

Go through this buffet line of Free Money options and try them all out. Just because you get money from one source does not mean you are done. Try another chapter. Does it appeal to you? Does it apply to you?

Not everything will. I don't know anyone who goes through a buffet line and takes from every single dish provided. The idea of a buffet is that there is

> The idea of a buffet is that there is something for everyone.

something for everyone, not everything for everyone. But if you do get something from every single chapter of this book, I certainly want to hear about it!

Get Excited

I get excited about all my projects, but I have to admit, I am really excited about this one. I know that times are tough, and a little extra cash is even more welcome right now. But even in times of plenty, this money could be yours. It also excites me that we have success stories from everyday people who used the methods of the first Free Money book. Maybe I should have busted from the starting gates with their stories. But if you know me, you know I like to talk. Those stories are up next.

I want you to be excited about the possibilities of Free Money. Those two words alone do it for me.

Believe it or not, some people have a hard time accepting Free Money. Think of it like this… it was yours to begin with and some-one is simply returning it to you. In some cases, that is exactly what happens. The unclaimed assets database actually has funds with the owner's name on it. If there were an old account somewhere with five bucks or five hundred bucks, why in the world would you say no to it? If you are eligible for a government grant because you meet the criteria, that money should go to you. That money is intended to help people, so take it with a smile.

I know most of you are not so shy about Free Money. I know most of you are chomping at the bit to find some Free Money.

Enough of me blabbering. Let's do it!

The number one concern on people's minds when they pick up a book like this boils down to three words: Will it work?

These methods to find Free Money really do work. As I said, they worked for me, but I also know that some people are skeptics. I can say anything, but hearing it from other people makes it real.

It is real.

The event that probably tickles me the most is not the success stories of the big dollar getters, although that is tremendously exciting. The stories that I love most are the ones that started right here.

When you are watching television and see me talking about the books, you know that when you call to order, you are going to talk to someone in our call center. The guys and gals who take your orders were so intrigued with the Free Money ideas that they decided to try the methods, too.

And guess what? These methods worked. The customer service employees tested the book for themselves, unbeknownst to me, and got results. To be able to chat with customers and tell them that these methods really do work is priceless. Maybe they should be the ones to go on television and talk about the book.

The call center in Pueblo, Colorado is buzzing with success stories from employees who have profited from the Free Money book. Here are just a few examples to get the party started.

> Cindy: "Free Money was great! I felt like I was looking for buried treasure and I found it! It is something you want to share with everyone you know. It was like I was on a mission! I found $277 for my brother, and $66 for my brother-in-law. You should try it for yourself and see who you can find Free Money for!"
>
> Dan: "If it had not been for the easy instructions provided, I would not have been aware of the $400 that

was unclaimed, but in my name. I had no idea and I had no idea how to find it until the Free Money book."

Jerri: "I totally love the Free Money book. I have found money for several family members and friends. I found over $200 for my sister, and over $1,300 for my father-in-law."

Jacki: "Talk about being surprised! I really did have some unclaimed money waiting for me to claim. I was so excited that I started calling other family members to let them know."

It is exciting, but obviously not everyone will have unclaimed money. It depends on each person's circumstances and situations, but it will work for millions of people who have money waiting for them. In addition, we have found that even if it doesn't work for you, you should check for your friends, family members, and other folks in your life. Who knows what exciting finds there could be out there?

People are shocked when they find their name or the name of a family member who has Free Money waiting for them out there. It lights a fire. They keep searching the database to make sure everyone they know does not have any money out there that they don't know about.

Can you imagine the thrill of calling your mother and telling her that you found some Free Money for her?

There are many success stories with HUGE dollars. No bull, I am talking HUGE! Hang on to your hats; some of these stories and the figures will blow you away! Let's look at a gal who has had huge success finding Free Money. Lisette is an average person with no college education. She is now a MILLIONAIRE.

Talk about results!

Lisette decided to dabble and take a chance. She had no real estate experience and she is living proof that applying these methods in the books can have miraculous rewards. The economy is suf-

> "I made over $1,000,000."
> —Lisette Kremer

fering, but in that reality there is also a silver lining. The numbers of foreclosures that are out there are ripe for the picking. Lisette knows how to pick them.

By "doing foreclosures" as she calls it, she has made a million dollars! We'll give you her story.

There are different ways to "do foreclosures" as you will learn. You can buy and sell to make a quick profit. You can buy and live in the property. You can buy and rent it out and have residual income every month.

One gal, Nora, applied these Free Money methods. She has told the Free Money offices that she has made close to $2 million. She was unsure, of course, at first. But she tried and that first taste of success made her realize that these methods can work and get great results. We'll give you her story, too.

In addition, we hear from folks all the time who have read my books and apply the tips and techniques, who are astounded with their results. Some are thrilled to discover $600 in Free Money; some get a kick out of $6,000 coming their way. Some are thrilled to be on the receiving end of $43,000!

People get money from lost accounts, from easy ways to make $10K, from an inheritance they never knew about. This book is here to shed light on ways that you can find more money.

Another remarkable story that warms my heart that came to my attention is Tyrone. He was homeless and now he has the money for a college education and the career of his dreams. He now has money to live, and he has a life now.

He received money from Free Money sources and was able to get his life back on track and launch an electronics business. I love hearing stories like that of Tyrone, and love including such stories in my book when I hear about them. It just proves that the Free Money is out there. And yes, we'll tell you Tyrone's story, too.

Please be sure to let me know of other success stories you hear about, so I can include them in future editions of the book and in the Free Money newsletters.

Never say never. Free Money success stories happen all the time. These are real stories of real people who used the methods to find real money.

They all would use the same sentiment: "If it can happen for me, it can happen for you, too."

CHAPTER I

Free Money
for YOU

I hope I've been clear. There are Free Money programs and there are billions of dollars in these programs. Accept that much as fact... because it is.

The government should have a sign like the golden arches stating billions of dollars and millions served. The only thing separating you from the millions who received their share of the money is that they asked for it.

You now know that you MUST ask for it. Just like the lottery, you can't win unless you play; you can't get a grant or money from these programs using our Free Money methods unless you try and apply.

As I said earlier, we can't list every grant possibility in this book. There are approximately 4,000 government programs, both federal and state, as well as local programs. Listing them all would kill a lot of trees.

We'll tell you where to go to find them, but it's up to you to apply.

Private Places, Too

Maybe I raised some eyebrows with the mention of "private places." All I convey is that there are private sources of Free Money, too, not just government programs. Private foundations also give away loads of money.

There are thousands of independent private organizations and sources of money available to individuals. Just like government programs, you have to apply. They have their funding, and they have their criteria. If you meet said criteria, turn in your application.

As was written in the first Free Money book: "In 2008, 20 million people got Free Money from some of these sources. But guess what? MILLIONS MORE QUALIFY."

I did not bother to update that stat because that point has not changed. Millions of people are aware of these sources and tap into these funds. But millions more have never heard of them and could get their hands on this Free Money, too.

You very well could be among the millions who are entitled to some of this Free Money. The odds are in your favor. I was shocked to learn that even I had Free Money out there.

How It Works

The private foundations are obviously funded privately. Rich folks, or charitable folks looking to do some good, donate to these foundations to spread the wealth and make the world a little better.

If you are inclined, you could start a foundation and give Free Money grants to whatever cause that moves you. Maybe you want to help women small business owners, or basket weavers or inner city basketball coaches. It does not matter. The funds would be provided to those who fulfill the requirements and apply for the money.

With government programs, it operates a little differently. The source of the funding is a big mixed up game. It's not as simple as a private foundation declaring, "We have money for this cause."

In Washington, it gets very convoluted. Congress and your senators and your representatives pass bills that include extra little "attachments" in them. It's a big messy game of Let's Make a Deal. Someone says, "I will vote yes to pass this bill, BUT in order to get my yes vote, I will throw a sentence into the bill so I get something in return."

> These billions of dollars in these programs are your tax dollars at work.

The bill becomes full of back and forth deals, and the original bill gets lost in all the wheeling and dealing. Government allocations are rarely logical or reasonable. It is all: "what you can do for me," "you owe me," and "we had a deal."

Your senator may vote yes on a certain bill because, included in the bill, he gets money for his state to have a program for grants. The grants could be for some specific minority, employment field or special cause.

The senator gets bragging rights that he brought home funds for home repair grants, scholarships or research programs. But while he's busy patting himself on the back, the folks that could benefit from this legislation are not specifically notified and most are left in the dark.

Let's shine the light.

Earmarks

I don't think it has to be so complicated, but that is how Washington operates. The extra stuff that gets put in a bill is usually called pork. The other term you hear is earmark. Funds are earmarked for a certain purpose. It's all a big game. Pork. Earmarks. Let's Make A Deal. A simple piece of legislation rarely exists. With everything that gets thrown in the mix, a thick bulky bill is usually the norm.

These little paddings add up. Billions of dollars are tucked in as a bill makes its way around Capitol Hill. It is out of control and this way of doing business has increased tremendously in the past decade.

It becomes a big giant swirling monster. With the advent of funds getting directed here, there and everywhere, the presence of lobbyists has become part of the culture. The lobbyists storm Washington trying to persuade their senators into earmarking funds for their pet projects.

The corruption and political favors are rampant. I could go off on a rant, but the point of all this discussion is simple. BILLIONS of dollars are sitting in the government coffers.

Get Yours

If you are eligible for that money, don't you want to know about it? Of course you do. But those bills are monster pieces of paperwork that no one wants to read… not even the legislators messing around with them.

Here's the sweet part. You don't have to read the bills. You don't even need to understand how government programs came to be.

All you need to know is that the government has a lot of programs, and it would be a shame not to apply to those that fit you.

This book has no hidden agenda. It tells it like it is and lays it all out. It gives you a quick, simple, easy to read book that lights the way to show how to pursue these programs.

Let's go. It's time to get your fair share of this Free Money.

Quick Ways to Free Money

I give you a choice. Do you want to read through thousands of government programs and try to figure out what may apply to you? Or do you want to be able to sort first and then read only what matters to you? Yeah, I thought so.

The sorting is done. The simplifying is done. This Free Money book saves you time and money by giving you easy access to the latest Free Money opportunities.

In addition to this book, the one other item you need is the Internet. Our world is wired and the data that lives in cyber space is data that can translate to real money in the real world in your real pocket.

If you do not have Internet access at home, that's okay. Go to a friend or family member or you can go to your local library and use their free Internet. The fastest, easiest way to do this Free Money stuff is using the Internet, so take advantage of the speed and ease.

There are millions of people who are entitled to this Free Money and billions

> The fastest, easiest way to do this free money stuff is certainly using the internet.

of dollars out there, and you could be in the running for some of it! I got some, and you are just as likely to get some.

It blows my mind how much money is just sitting there and new sources and new grants are popping up all the time, but hardly anyone has a clue. This is why you should subscribe to the monthly FREE MONEY newsletters… to keep you current on the opportunities out there.

If you haven't done so already, get your phone and call customer service now and get on the mailing list for the latest, up-to-date resources and information via the monthly newsletters. You can take comfort in knowing that you're up to speed on ways to keep Free Money flowing into your life. Who knows, you just might end up talking to Cindy, Dan or Jacki, or one of the other call center folks who used the Free Money book to get a piece of the action.

I want to make sure that relevant, current information continues to come your way. The best investments are the ones we make in ourselves. Staying in touch with Free Money makes sense (and cents).

Make the call now and start earning Free Money fast! 1-888-445-5206.

CHAPTER 2

Free Money Inspiration

Being the creatures we are, we love to see others who have gone before us who can show us the way. We like to see what's possible before we begin. We all like a little inspiration to light our path.

I already mentioned some names. Let me give you their stories so you can see that this Free Money stuff is the real deal.

It brightens our day at the Free Money headquarters when we get word that these methods reap big results for our readers. But it doesn't matter if someone learned of these methods in my books or simply used the same methods. The gist is the same… these methods work!

One gal who used the methods in this book told us that she honestly didn't know where she would be or what she would be doing if not for the Free Money methods she discovered.

Lisette Kramer made more than a million dollars using the methods you'll learn in this book. One deposit alone was almost $750,000. That's what I call astounding results!

She is not a real estate broker and had no real estate experience. She had no college education. She was just like millions of Americans who go to work every day and come home tired and try to take care of their kids. She wanted more time with her kids, so she decided to try out making money in foreclosures.

> Lisette has continued to learn and grow in this method of buying foreclosures.

She knew of a lot of foreclosed properties and started to think that maybe she had the guts to try out a Free Money tactic. She took this information and ran with it and saw herself as an investor. Now she sees herself as a businesswoman who works from home and has more time to spend with her kids.

That's what this is all about. Freedom. Lisette now loves the freedom to be able to be with her kids, take them to the zoo or just spend real, quality time with them.

How did she do it?

Real estate foreclosures and having faith in herself to do it.

Lisette confided that she was nervous at first. In the beginning, she had someone help her who was familiar with buying houses and looking for foreclosures. Now she finds them herself by going online, looking in newspapers, attending auctions and asking different sources. There's a lot of word of mouth and, as she says it, "there's tons of opportunity out there now. Now is the time to do it."

She now works with foreclosed properties to make her money instead of going to a job. She buys foreclosures and fixes them up. Lisette likes to work with her hands and does a lot of the work herself. Sometimes she rents them out for cash flow and sometimes she sells them for a quick flip.

When she bought her first property, Lisette used some money she received when her parents died. Lisette said, "My parents died and left some money, there were some accounts that I found and that helped me, initially, to purchase my first house. After that, when I made money, I was like, wow! This is faster than having to work for an entire year, I made more money in two months than I would have made in a whole year doing the work I was doing before."

Lisette still gets excited talking about the first time she made money. She recounts telling her friend, "Check this out! I had this condo for three months and I kept it and rented it for three months and I made three thousand dollars in three months. I just sold it, I just put it on the market and sold it, and here is my check for $40,000!"

She didn't stop there. Lisette continued to learn and grow in this method of buying foreclosures. One deal reaped her a deposit check for $747,000!

Using web sites to cross-check the value of properties to ensure she was buying at the best low price, Lisette became comfortable buying foreclosed properties. "Then you just fix it up and you follow the guidelines and the building code regulations, which are pretty simple. A lot of people are afraid at first, but once you get into it, there's always a way to fix it."

Lisette claims it's a very easy process. Sometimes she goes in with others to buy a property, too. She says it has changed her life. "There was a time I really didn't have a life, but now I can do anything that I want. Anything is possible. All you need is the desire, and then you do it. You might say at first, "I can't do it," or "It can't be done." Just have a positive attitude, and you'll see it can be done."

Lisette took an initial investment and bought a foreclosed property at a good price. The rest is history. Renting and fixing up and selling foreclosed real estate have become her passion. She met other people and now invests in other properties with them. Her first transaction was all it took to get her ball rolling. And it doesn't look like she is going to stop anytime soon.

Lisette learned by doing. She learned how to buy a property, how to fix it up to meet code and how to sell. She also learned she likes having rental properties giving steady monthly income.

She says the most important thing she learned is this… don't be afraid to try the Free Money methods.

Real Grants for Real People

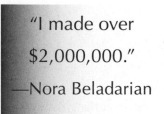

"I made over $2,000,000."
—Nora Beladarian

Another gal made millions using another one of the methods of Free Money… grants. She actually started applying for grants before reading Free Money and proclaims the valuable information in this book is indeed right on the money. She says she wishes Kevin would have written these books years ago, but she's thrilled they are here now.

Yes, Nora Beladarian has received more than two million dollars in grant money! The first grant she received was $5,000, and she was amazed at how easy it was to earn that Free Money.

A favorite story she likes to tell is when she applied for another grant that was going to be $62,000 a year for three years. She got a call from the grant office and they upped it to $100,000 a year!

Nora says that grants have funded her projects over the past decade or so, and the running total to date is just over two million dollars. She absolutely loves her work, and being able to pursue her passion with funds that never have to be paid back is a dream come true.

Is applying for grants difficult? Nora says no. She says it can be tedious providing all the information, but it's worth it. Nora explains that different grants have different restrictions and time-lines. She once learned of a grant she wanted to apply for at 4:00 pm on a Thursday, but applications were due at noon on Friday. She stayed up all night to write the application, but her time was well spent. She got the money.

The grants she receives for her work are not paid in one lump sum. They start on a set date and payments are made monthly. Nora states that her grant funders want a monthly reporting of her project, which she gladly provides because she wants to share the progress of her work. She's grateful for those monthly checks… monthly checks she never has to pay back!

Nora's passion is focused on the abuse of children and adults with disabilities. She continues to find government and private funding sources for her projects. The biggest lump sum to date she received is $500,000. Nora says, of course, she will continue to apply for more grants. Absolutely!

All grants are different, and for her work, the money is paid to a non-profit agency. She partners with non-profits and they pay her to be the director of the programs. She has become very good at writing grants and, if she has questions about the budget portion, she always finds someone to ask and she easily gets help.

Nora says that, for her, a grant application is explaining what the project is, what she will do and what amount she needs to fund it. It is a written application with a budget, and most applications are done online. She says notification of approval is usually very quick and monthly payments are always promptly paid. Nora has received money from many sources and some, like the Department of Justice, pay right away, within 24 hours.

> **Regular monthly checks that never have to be paid back!**

She says the tricky part of grants is finding the money being offered. That's why she thinks the Free Money books are so great. Take a quick peek at the chapters at the back of this book and you'll see all kinds of Free Money sources. She also suggests using the web sites like www.grants.gov. Nora says you may see terms like RFP which simply means Request For Proposal. Write up your proposal and send it off.

To keep her on target and keep her focused when writing a grant, Nora writes down three goals or tasks she thinks are important in her work with abused children and adults with disabilities and the cost of those three goals. She crafts that into a proposal and waits to receive the grant award letter.

She states that many grant applications are just filling in the blanks and answering the questions online, but even when she had to pull her all-nighter, it was still worth it. Would you give one night's work for $100,000 per year for three years? I thought you might.

Nora is grateful for the grant money and for how easily the Free Money book explains the process. She told our staffers that getting grant money has been absolutely fantastic for her because she has been able to really bring awareness of the problem of her clients to a national level. Grant money has allowed her to bring the message, the training, the skills and the materials to people who are responding to crime victims with disabilities in a better way. To do her life's work on someone else's dime is a thrill!

She points out that for her, grant writing is easy, but if someone is intimidated, many communities, libraries and local colleges offer free or dirt-cheap grant writing classes.

Nora told our office: "I loved the Free Money book. I thought it was very clear and it described the steps to take to get grant money. It's exactly what I do to get the money I need for the work I do."

From a lady who has been able to get $2 million in grants, that is high praise.

From Homeless to Happy

Another gratifying success story came to us from Tyrone Clark. Tyrone learned about grants and it changed his life. Tyrone was homeless and now he's in a different state of life because of Free Money.

Tyrone was excited to share the Free Money methods that worked for him. He went from homeless to happy. He says, in a nutshell, that he went online and started researching scholarships. He filled out applications and wrote essays.

And then his phone started ringing.

> He didn't get just one scholarship; he got many.

His net-to-date in Free Money scholarships is $85,000. He says he used to be the guy rounding up shopping carts and bagging your stuff at one of the big box stores. Now Tyrone gives back to the community with volunteer work and community service and is grateful for the college scholarship money.

He didn't get just one scholarship; he got many. Gates Millennium Scholarship, Ace Award, Burger King Scholarship, Rosa Park Foundation, Push Excel and Horatio Alger. He was thrilled to get money to go to school. He's just as thrilled that it's all Free Money that he doesn't have to pay back.

Tyrone didn't have an easy life. His parents were embattled; his father was on drugs and was very abusive to his mother. Then she moved herself and Tyrone into another situation that was also abusive. Then she moved in with his aunt and Tyrone had nowhere to go. He was homeless. He went to the library to apply for scholarships online. Tyrone says he had no credit, so loans weren't the path for him. This Free Money was a tremendous blessing.

Our staffers asked Tyrone if the process was hard. He said, "not at all… you just have to do it." He went to the library to use the computer and filled out online applications. He says anyone should be able to do that. His Free Money paid for school, housing and books. It covered everything he needed, plus he got refunds back from the school because he had more than enough scholarship money. He was able to buy supplies and computer equipment to start his own company.

Tyrone is one grateful young man. He claims that if not for the Free Money scholarships, he would still be homeless and still be out there not really doing anything and wasting his life. Now he says he feels hope. He feels success. To have clothes and an apartment; he is thankful for his blessings.

His payouts have been many, including $10,000 and $14,000 and $20,000. Tyrone says the scholarship money first goes to the school (he was accepted at an art institute), and then the leftover is distributed to him for his living expenses. He feels like he hit the lotto jackpot.

What do you think? If Tyrone can get $85,000, do you think maybe you are able to try for some Free Money for college, too?

Free Money to the Rescue

How about one more inspirational success story? Remember, these folks are ordinary everyday folks, just like you. They have no superpowers. All they did was use the methods we describe in the Free Money books.

Zoila Perusset was having a hard go of it. Business declined and she was having trouble with her mortgage. She was struggling on every level, not just financially. The death of her husband hit her hard.

Because of the Free Money book, Zoila was happy to learn that there were programs for people going through rough times. Programs like those offered through HUD are getting her through.

With loan modification, Zoila's monthly housing payment dropped dramatically. She was thrilled to learn that she could get a reduced payment that also includes the taxes and the insurance, too. She told our staffers, "Because of Kevin's book, I learned that I could save about $24,000 a year!"

Zoila was overjoyed to be able to keep her house and have her kids be able to stay in their home. "The fear was horrible," she told us. Not knowing what to do, where to go, who to talk to, and all the time fearing she was going to lose her home. Learning about loan modifications in the Free Money book changed her life and that of her kids. Zoila also learned about health insurance options for her children and is overjoyed to have low cost coverage for her three kids. Right out of the book… Healthy Families program… Zoila was able to save $500 a month doing so!

Her words of thanks for the Free Money books, "I am extremely happy and so relieved. To feel this relief is huge, like 200 pounds were lifted off of me. I forgot how it feels to feel good."

Zoila commented that she doesn't read a lot of books, but is grateful for Kevin's books. She said they are so easy to read and that all the information she needed was right in the book. She went to the web sites listed. It is as easy as opening her laptop, with a cup of coffee and the Free Money book, and just getting started.

She also confided in our team that she has a lot of debt and she had a hard time sleeping at night because of the worry. That was when she turned on the TV in the wee hours of the night and learned of our books. She now says that reading Kevin's books gave her peace of mind, knowing she would be able to wipe out her debt.

As a single mother, Zoila calls these books her partner. She is thrilled to be finding answers and solutions. Zoila was even able to find more Free Money help to save $4,000 a year in her water and utility bills.

Her testimonial is really amazing:

"Thanks to Kevin's book, I was able to research and find out that myself, being a widow, I was able to claim benefits

for the children. Every month the kids get a check from the Social Security of $865 per month. And thanks to the money, I'm able to survive. It's money that is needed to pay my expenses at home, my groceries, for the three kids. After reading the book, I realized that I was able to get approximately $26,000 a year for the children through Social Security. And that money, basically, is the money that is paying my bills right now. And that's money that I didn't know about until I was able to find out through Kevin's book.

"If we didn't have that money we wouldn't be here. Simple as that. There was no way I could've stayed in this house. No way. Being a single mother is extremely difficult. The decisions are all mine. There's no one to share any decision making so I have to make sure that whatever decision I make is the right one. Losing my husband was horrible. Still is. There are times that I feel very lonely and I'm sure the kids feel the same, but there's always hope. There's always hope and I guess through this, through Kevin's book, it brought me a lot of relief and peace of mind. I have the book on my nightstand. I refer to it when I need to. And I'm thankful for that."

I always am delighted to hear from folks and what they have to say about "Kevin's books," but stories like this especially matter. Helping folks through their hard times is priceless. Being able to put out information in a book that helps people every day is what we do.

These stories are meant to inspire you and show that ordinary everyday people read these books, try these methods and have success. We try to keep it from being too complicated. We try to tell it straight. We try to give you good information.

We think we succeeded.

Do you want to share a story that will inspire others? Send it in. Free Money stories make the world go 'round.

Now, start reading and get busy finding Free Money.

CHAPTER 3

Overview of Sources

There's not just one source of Free Money. For example, there are thousands of government programs—there are thousands of them. I also love government grants… Free Money from the government that you never have to pay back. I also love all the other areas of Free Money that we will explore. Keep reading and you'll feel like a kid in a candy store with so much to choose from and it all looks sweet.

Before we get to the details of how to find this Free Money, I want to open your eyes to all the possibilities. For example, we will talk about unclaimed assets. This source is money that is yours that has been locked away and no one told you it was there.

The list of possibilities within the realm of unclaimed funds alone seems endless. Let me whet your appetite. It's possible that you have money in:

- ✔ Bank accounts
- ✔ Credit unions
- ✔ Accounts from failed banks and savings and loans

- ✔ Minor child accounts
- ✔ Christmas Club accounts
- ✔ Credit balances from loans
- ✔ Unredeemed CDs
- ✔ Insurance policies naming you as beneficiary
- ✔ Group life insurance policies
- ✔ Accident and health payments
- ✔ Life insurance policies on mortgages or credit cards
- ✔ Worker comp benefits
- ✔ Social Security benefits
- ✔ Union benefits
- ✔ Uncashed government checks
- ✔ Undeliverable income and property tax refunds
- ✔ Undistributed property tax refunds
- ✔ FHA mortgage insurance premium overpayments
- ✔ PMI refunds
- ✔ Unclaimed inheritances
- ✔ Lost stock certificates
- ✔ Uncashed interest or dividends
- ✔ Shares from stock splits
- ✔ Unredeemed bonds
- ✔ Stock dividends
- ✔ Unrefunded utility deposits
- ✔ Unrefunded credit balances
- ✔ Unused sick or vacation pay
- ✔ Expense account reimbursements
- ✔ Pension and profit sharing payments
- ✔ Severance pay
- ✔ Employee savings and medical accounts
- ✔ Death benefits
- ✔ Unredeemed casino winnings
- ✔ Unused gift certificates

✔ Undistributed IRAs

✔ Amounts held in bankruptcy court never claimed by creditors

✔ Refundable court fees

✔ Class action lawsuit settlements

✔ Credit balances on any accounts

✔ Undistributed proceeds or assets from estate sales

✔ Residuals

✔ Royalty payments

✔ Prepaid cards

✔ Uncashed money orders or travelers checks

✔ Rebates

We're just getting started. There are tax refunds and tax credits. There are funds and foundations. There are no-interest loans and grants. There are ways to get money out of your house. There are ways to get free services, which is the same as getting Free Money. There are ways to make $10K fast. The Free Money possibilities in real estate are endless. Free Money sources go on and on.

> ...there is the reality that free money sources go on and on.

Maybe you'll discover an inheritance you had no idea was coming your way. Maybe you'll discover that you have money from a previous employer. Maybe you'll discover that your house is a gold mine. Perhaps you will find Free Money in some new unexpected source.

I hear from people all the time. They were so skeptical and then they become total Free Money converts. Some of the methods here may be a one-time thing. If you discover that you are the heir to a million dollar inheritance, I doubt you will be disappointed that it is only one inheritance.

There are other ways to Free Money that you can do over and over. This is your book. Play with it and discover all the possible Free Money sources that could work for you.

Go have some fun.

CHAPTER 4

Bank Accounts

We all know the thrill of finding lost money. Admit it... finding a quarter on the pavement or on the floor of the mall or airport excites the kid in you. Most people have experienced the unexpected delight of putting on a jacket or pair of pants that haven't been worn in months and finding money in the pockets. It could be a twenty-dollar bill, or even a single, and you get that sense of woo-hoo! Free Money!

Money that comes to us unexpectedly gives a Free Money good vibe. Imagine finding a whole jackpot of surprise Free Money. It's possible, and more probable than you may think.

Forgotten but Not Gone

This is a turn around of the old phrase, gone but not forgotten. Some people and things will leave us, and we will miss them and never forget them. This Free Money source is the opposite. There could be money out there with your name on it that has been forgotten, but it's not gone. It's still sitting and waiting for you to claim it.

Bank accounts are one common source of Free Money. There are many ways to have a stash of Free Money you're not aware of.

Inactive bank accounts are very common and a great gift of Free Money.

- ✔ Maybe you had a bank account set up by your folks when you were a kid.

- ✔ Maybe Grandma gave you an account when you went to college.

- ✔ Maybe you had an account when you just starting your first job, or as a newlywed or starting a family.

> Inactive bank accounts are very, very common and a great gift of free money.

You could have an old account from any number of sources. There are also dozens of reasons why these accounts fall off your radar and end up in that wasteland of "lost money."

Maybe you moved. Maybe you changed jobs. Maybe you got divorced. Maybe there was the death of a spouse or a family member.

I know people who had accounts they never knew about that were set up for them by parents or grandparents. Granny put in a birthday deposit every year planning to surprise you on the 18th birthday, but Granny passed before that date. The recipient never knew an account even existed.

And here's a big one… maybe the bank changed names and account numbers so many times, you lost track.

Banks are continuously getting bought out, merged, consolidated or taken over. Think of the bank on a prominent corner in your town. How many times has it changed names? I thought so. You probably can't remember all the names it's carried.

With the changes that banks go through and the changes that people go through, it's not surprising that bank accounts fall through the cracks. A bank may consider your account inactive if you do not make a deposit or a withdrawal within a certain number of months. Some banks consider the account abandoned if you have no activity within one year.

Another way bank accounts go missing is when the banks themselves go under. We've had a lot of that in recent years. Banks failed in almost epic proportion. The number of closings started to rival the failed banks of the Great Depression.

When a bank fails, you still have rights to your accounts. That is why we place our trust in FDIC insured accounts. We want our money to be safe. When a bank closes, sometimes the FDIC issues out the funds to account holders at that time. Sometimes, the money is transferred to another bank or a custodian account is set up. The point is… the account still exists and still has your name on it.

Certainly, if it were your primary account, you probably wouldn't lose track of it. But if it was a smaller account, it could fall off your radar if you had a lot of stuff swirling in your life. Furthermore, if that account were set up for you by another family member, it would be even easier for it to fade away.

So you can see… there are many reasons for people having inactive bank accounts, and this source gives those same people the chance at Free Money.

Searching for Lost Treasure

In order to locate old bank accounts and the other Free Money sources we will cover, you have to go on a treasure hunt. The hunt is made easier by the friend you have in the Internet. It's better than an ancient treasure map.

Without getting out of your seat, you can uncover treasure that's been buried for years. Lost bank accounts are just one part of the loot. The larger picture is called "unclaimed assets," and we will break that down later, asset by asset.

There is a simple beauty in these kinds of searches. All you do is type in some basic information and search features, and the online databases will do all the "Indiana Jones" hunting for you. If you want swashbuckling adventure, you can watch a movie while you are searching these unclaimed assets databases.

To my knowledge, there isn't a single, all-encompassing database of every possible source of lost income, but there is something that comes pretty close. I'll get to that in a minute.

Let me clarify one last point. Successful searches for unclaimed assets require that you dip back into your memory bank and use common sense. When you are searching these systems, you need to be sharp. You need to use every advantage, which means you should type in all the names by which you have ever been known.

- ✔ Current name
- ✔ Maiden name
- ✔ Previous married names
- ✔ Middle names
- ✔ Initials
- ✔ Nicknames
- ✔ Common misspellings of your name
- ✔ Jr. or Sr.

You get the idea. If Granny opened an account for you when you were small, it will not be under your married name. Perhaps you were not consistent when setting up accounts. Maybe your name is Walter Edward Johnson, but you have always gone by Edward Johnson… or, maybe W. Edward Johnson… or, W.E. Johnson. You get my drift. Use any and all combinations that could be attached to money in your name.

You should also search every state that you ever lived in or worked in, and those of your relatives who may have opened an account for you. Often, these lost accounts were set up in New York and Delaware banks.

Yep, crazy as it sounds, you could have money in states that you never thought about. Every state (and good old Washington, D.C.) maintains its own system and database for this stash of unclaimed cash. Millions of people have this missing cash out there with their names on it, and they simply don't know to ask for it.

> You can search under your name, a family name, or the name of a business.

So let your fingers do the walking. You can even play the theme song to "Raiders of the Lost Ark" while you are doing your searches.

Where do you start to look for this lost treasure? One good site is www.unclaimed.com. Once you start to play around on this site, you will see all the possible sources of unclaimed Free Money. It's very exciting.

Since this chapter talks about old bank accounts, you can go right to that database and check your name (make sure to check all of your possible names and all your possible states), and see what you come up with.

I like how this site explains things and how easy it is to get around. Give it a test run at www.unclaimed.com/lostbankaccount.htm. Here is my only misgiving. They do charge a small fee to conduct the search for lost bank or credit union accounts. If you ever read any of my stuff, you know that I do not like to pay fees. However, I think finding money outweighs the hassle of a small charge.

With that being said, if I can avoid a fee, I always do. So let me tell you about the National Association of Unclaimed Property Administrators, or NAUPA. The name is long, but wow, you will love this association.

Remember when I mentioned the possibility of an all-encompassing, single-source search tool? This source is about as close as we are going to get, but let me tell you, the getting is good. To see for yourself, go to www.missingmoney.org, the web site of the NAUPA. They are also found at www.unclaimed.org, which gets a little confusing since we just mentioned www.unclaimed.com. Here's why; the dot org does not charge a fee.

This web site strives to include as many sources of money and property as humanly possible. The site is updated monthly and it is FREE to use. It doesn't get any better than updated and free!

To get started, enter your name and state in the space on the first screen.

Now, click.

Results appear immediately. The information box identifies the state in which the money is held, the last known address, the company or holder of the money and the amount. It will show either more than $100, less than $100, or unknown.

To all the folks at NAUPA—we love you!

You can search under your name, a family name, or the name of a business. If the personal account is in your name, of course, you can claim that money. If you are the business owner, you, too, can claim the money. If the money is in the name of a family member and you are a legal heir, you can also claim the money.

If the money is under mom's name and mom is still alive and kicking, won't she be surprised when she finds out she has Free Money! Once you get clicking, you are going to keep clicking. You'll never get tired of finding Free Money.

I swear this is the fastest magic I have ever seen to find your lost money. This was the method that our call center folks first tried because it was so easy, and because it produces results.

I am well aware that some people out there are skeptical. I have two words for you: Try it! Any agency or company that owes you money is probably in this database. This is a substantial database and it continually gets updated each month.

I was like you, thinking there was no way I would have any lost money in my name... but then I tried it. With my slow finger typing, I pecked my name into the big beautiful database. In less than thirty seconds, it was magic. I discovered I had money due me!

My friends are all trying this fabulous method and the results are stunning. Some nice sums are showing up. But even if you're like my friend Nick and just get fifty bucks, don't you still want your fifty bucks? You bet you do!

You should lay claim to any money that is rightfully yours... because it's YOURS. Don't let it languish any longer in these unclaimed asset accounts. Times are tough and you have every right to collect every penny that is due you.

> Any agency or company that owes you money is probably in this database.

Even if you're a millionaire in want of nothing, the money is still yours. If you want to give it to charity once you receive it, that's your business. Do with it what you will. Just do it! Lay your hands on this newly found lost treasure!

If you do not find missing money here, the NAUPA people also link to state unclaimed property pages, and they also have "other links" that take you to federal agencies. I am not blowing smoke here. The Wall Street Journal has reported that there is nearly $33 billion of unclaimed cash and property sitting in the coffers of state governments.

Wow! $33 billion is a lot of smackaroos and some of that could be yours. It could belong to your deceased relatives, which means it could be yours. It could be from an old business of yours, which means it could be yours. You have absolutely nothing to lose by giving it a try.

If you find a match, you need to file a claim to collect the money. The directions are right on the site. Basically, you have to fill out a form for the state and provide identification that you are the person owed that money. It's a no brainer.

The state will then process your claim and send you a check. You don't usually know the exact amount, only the ballpark range, until the check arrives. Getting a nice chunk of change can be a sweet surprise!

Let me say it again. It's free to use the NAUPA site, so what are you waiting for? Go on and give it a whirl. Let me give you that URL again: www.missingmoney.org.

I'll be waiting for you in the next chapter. Take your time searching out that lost treasure. Have fun and good luck!

CHAPTER 5

Unclaimed Assets

Found money stories. Lost money stories. Free Money stories. Call it what you will, I love it!

Many Sources

This one area of Free Money is always a favorite. People are fascinated that this source exists. We always assume that we know what we having coming to us. We always assume we could never overlook any money that is due us. Well, we should never assume.

Many, MANY people discover unclaimed assets.

When you visit the web site, you will see that there is so much more out there than just forgotten bank accounts. There are several sources of Free Money available if we go looking:

- ✔ Safe deposit boxes
- ✔ Stocks, bond, mutual funds and dividends
- ✔ CDs
- ✔ Uncashed checks and wages
- ✔ Escrow accounts
- ✔ Trust funds
- ✔ Insurance policies
- ✔ Deposits with utility companies

The database is bursting with possibilities. Who would have thought maybe the phone company owed you a deposit from long, long ago? People discover these little treasures every day. The real treasure to remember is web sites like www.missingmoney.com.

These facts about unclaimed property come from the folks at NAUPA.

[www.unclaimed.org/what/]

We included this for the first Free Money book and the site remains unchanged on these facts:

✔ Every U.S. state, District of Columbia, Puerto Rico, the U.S. Virgin Islands—and Quebec, British Columbia and Alberta in Canada have unclaimed property programs that actively and continuously find owners of lost and forgotten assets.

✔ Unclaimed property laws have been around since the 1930s, but have become much broader and more enforced in the last 25 years. Unclaimed property is one of the original consumer protection programs.

✔ 2.5 million claims totaling $2.25 billion returned to rightful owners in FY2011 as a result of state unclaimed property program efforts. Amount of average claim: $892.

✔ $41.7 billion waiting to be returned by state unclaimed property programs.

✔ Claims can be made into perpetuity in most cases—even by heirs.

There is generally no deadline to lay claim to any money. If the property is yours, it is yours and you have the right to it. It will keep sitting there waiting for you until you go searching for it. You and everyone you know should go looking.

Unclaimed Property Defined

The National Association for Unclaimed Property Administrators states:

> "Unclaimed property" (sometimes referred to as "abandoned property") refers to accounts in financial institutions and companies that have had no activity generated or contact with the owner for one year or a longer period.

> "Common forms of unclaimed property include savings or checking accounts, stocks, uncashed dividends or payroll checks, refunds, traveler's checks, trust distributions, unredeemed money orders or gift certificates (in some states), insurance payments or refunds and life insurance policies, annuities, certificates of deposit, customer overpayments, utility security deposits, mineral royalty payments and contents of safe deposit boxes.

> [www.unclaimed.org/what/]

> "All the information is accessible free of charge by searching the state databases or MissingMoney..."

Each state has laws that protect you, the consumer. They prevent the company or bank from taking over your money. It is your money, plain and simple.

They, the business owners, are required to turn over the money or property to the state authorized official who becomes the keeper of the lost loot.

If the lost loot is stuff and not money, states do not have the capacity or storage facilities to hang on to this stuff forever. What they do is hold auctions and the money received for your item is then held for you. States, so I am told, do actively try to find the rightful owners of the dough. Even if they don't, I know that they DO work with NAUPA to update the www.missingmoney.com database. That, my friends, can literally mean Free Money for you.

> **There is generally no deadline to lay claim to any money.**

And I quote: "All the information is accessible free of charge by searching the state databases or MissingMoney.com or by contacting any state unclaimed property office." Beware… there will always be someone wanting to charge you for what you can get for free. It doesn't mean that you should pay for it.

You should contact institutions that hold your money or property every year and especially when there is an address change or change in marital status. For security reasons, most financial institutions do not forward mail. Keep accurate financial records and record all insurance policies, bank account numbers with bank names and addresses, types of accounts, stock certificates and rent and utility deposits.

- ✔ Cash all checks for dividends, wages, and insurance settlements without delay.

- ✔ Respond to requests for confirmation of account balances and stockholder proxies.

- ✔ If you have a safe deposit box, record its number, bank name and address, and give the extra key to a trusted person.

- ✔ Finally, prepare and file a will detailing the disposition of your assets.

[www.unclaimed.org/what/]

Be sure to tell your friends and family members about this amazing resource. There are countless numbers of people who could benefit from learning about this site.

Success Stories

The first Free Money book included these snippets:

MSNBC reported in March 2009 that California had $5 billion in unclaimed cash. One man, George of San Jose, used this web site and found $5,800 of his money.

The state of Oregon has $250 million in their treasure chest of unclaimed money. The Department of State spokesperson says that one in four Oregon residents have money in that chest.

The state of Washington collected $100 million in unclaimed loot in 2008.

The news reporter who reported the story on the unclaimed assets in Oregon and Washington used the unclaimed.org web site and discovered that she had Free Money waiting for her, too. There's no better substantiation for a news story than that.

South Carolina's program is called the Palmetto Payback. They actively search for the owners of abandoned accounts and unclaimed property. In 2008, they gave back over $12 million. One lucky individual received over $76,000!

In February of 2011, Palmetto Payback Program made the news again. They have a staff of ten people who seek the owners of the missing money. They find around 13,000 lucky owners each year according to a local South Carolina news station. On April 4, 2011, they paid someone more than $66,000. It was from an old life insurance policy.

In 2010, they paid back more than $2 million. They say they have 1.5 million accounts totaling about $300 million sitting in their coffers. $300 million, just in the state of South Carolina. What do you think your state has?

Those stories are timeless. Since we published the first Free Money book, success stories have poured in. As we stated in the beginning of this book, even our own customer service reps tried out this site and found their own missing money.

Thousands of people have come into Free Money because of learning of this quick and easy method. You have nothing to lose but a few minutes of your time. Give it a go.

Escheat

I don't want to complicate the issue, I just need to explain something. When talking about unclaimed property, you may come across the word "escheat." That is the legal word for the process that allows transfers of unclaimed property... from banks, credit unions, stock brokers, utility companies, employers, life insurance companies and all the other places that may end up with money and stuff that go unclaimed... to a government holding trust.

If you see the word escheat or an office or agency with that title, you know you're in the right place.

Free Money Shopping

Basically, that is what you are doing... shopping for Free Money. This book is better than any home shopping network. NAUPA is like a big mall that offers many boutiques to try. The NAUPA web site is one of my favorite places to hang out. They like to share the wealth and the information.

They even direct you to other sources for unclaimed property. Many of these sources will be covered in other places in this book, too. Some are things we might not have thought of; like frozen Swiss bank accounts. Seriously, there is a database to search for bank accounts and insurance accounts in other countries. If you go to the NAUPA page, they will have direct links to other pages. For example, here is a cut and paste from www.unclaimed.org/other/

Holocaust Links

Swiss Bankers Association

Victims of the Holocaust or their heirs can make claims to assets deposited in Swiss Banks during World War II.

Frozen Swiss Accounts Database Search Form

This web site provides a notice of claim procedures for locating Swiss, Swedish, French and British bank and insurance accounts.

Holocaust Claims Processing Office of the New York State Banking Department

This office attempts to recover assets deposited in European banks, monies never paid in connection with insurance policies issued by European insurers and lost or looted art for victims of the Holocaust.

The International Commission on Holocaust Era Insurance Claims

Search for unpaid insurance policies issued to victims of the Holocaust. Information is available in 23 languages.

The NAUPA site also gives international links to Bank of Canada, Australian Securities and Investments Commission, France Unclaimed Monies, New Zealand Unclaimed Monies and the Swiss Bankers Association.

Some of the other sites of possible Free Money sources include Federal Deposit Insurance Corporation, U.S. Federal Investments, Missing U.S. Federal Savings Bonds, U.S. Department of Housing and Urban Development, Veterans Administration Benefits, U.S. Railroad Retirement Board and the Pension Benefit Guaranty Corp.

The Pension Benefit Guaranty Corp. has a searchable database to determine whether you are owed any pension benefits, if your pension plan no longer exists because it was closed or was taken over by the pension agency. You also can track down the benefits if you are a survivor of the person who should be drawing the pension. This site will tell you what to do if you believe you are owed money, but aren't found in the agency's database.

> You may also search for free money that is in the name of your relatives.

You may also search for Free Money that is in the name of your relatives. Perhaps you have the records of your deceased relatives and there are bank statements from banks that no longer exist. You can contact the FDIC for help in tracing the history of a bank. They have a toll-free consumer hotline that you can call with any questions: 877-ASK-FDIC (275-3342). Visit www2.fdic.gov/funds/index.asp for more information.

If an account is more than ten years old, the funds are probably lumped in with unclaimed property at the state treasurer's office. That is something else you need to know. Each state can be contacted regarding unclaimed assets.

State Offices

Most people don't realize that states have unclaimed property offices. Did you know that all fifty states have a big lost and found department for this missing money? Many people have no clue.

My research team has done the homework for you. We created a list of each state office and the contact information. Refer to Appendix I to find your state or any state you have lived or worked in.

If you discover funds or property that you think belongs to you or a relative, fill out a claim form. To request a claim form, you have to go through the state in which the property is held. The state will need to verify that the asset or money belongs to you and that you are who you say you are.

You might want to do the search for family, too. Family members are often unaware that they are entitled to collect the unclaimed cash, property and benefits of their deceased relatives.

A lot of money from all kinds of sources goes unclaimed and thus goes to these state offices to sit. More than $22 billion is unclaimed every year and only about $1 billion finds its way home.

Do you think you could be entitled to a share of those billions?

You'll never know until you search. The sources of Free Money, missing money and lost money seem endless.

CHAPTER 6

Savings Bonds

The federal government has all types of money for us. An often-overlooked source is unclaimed savings bonds. As we were doing the re-write for this updated version of the Free Money book, most of this information still remains unchanged. If you have the first Free Money book, this chapter may read a little like déjà vu.

There's nothing wrong with hearing a good story twice. Reminders are always useful, especially, when it comes to stuff we've forgotten about. That seems like a brain teaser, but it's not. When it comes to Free Money tactics, reinforcement is a positive thing.

Let's reminisce.

Bonds

Many people have United States savings bonds they have long forgotten about. Maybe your grandmother had some years ago. Maybe your parents took some out for you when you were a kid. Maybe you bought some yourself and they simply got lost.

It is easy to misplace or forget about bonds. They are purchased and then tucked away, waiting for the maturity date when they can be cashed in. In the course of this book, I have asked friends if they have savings bonds. Most get a puzzled look and their eyes roll around in their heads as they try to recall if they have bonds and where those bonds might be.

One pal, Roger, knows he used to have them. In the early days of his career, he was a government employee and he had money taken out of each paycheck to buy bonds. It was an easy and simple savings plan for him.

> More than 55 million Americans have, or had, bonds.

Roger remembers cashing most of them in when he bought his first house, but he scratches his head at my question. "Now that you mention it, I remember that some of them were not at maturity yet so I couldn't cash them in. But for the life of me, I can't think of where they might be."

Roger is not alone. Many folks don't know if they still have outstanding matured bonds. Do you want to know if you fall into that category?

To see if you have matured bonds that have not been redeemed, go to unclaimedassets.com and read up. The numbers keep going up.

There was $12.5 billion in value of unclaimed savings bonds as of 2005. As of March 2009, the US Savings Bond Search page stated that the amount topped $15 billion.

As we go to press in January 2014, the number is now $16 billion.

$16 BILLION!

$16 billion in bonds. That equates to millions of actual bonds. Are you the holder of any of those millions of unclaimed bonds?

Bonds stop earning interest after forty years, but they are sitting there, waiting for their rightful owner to show up. People were gifted bonds, used their payroll deduction plans or just bought them outright. More than 55 million Americans have, or had, bonds.

Most government offices simply don't have the manpower, or the motivation, to track down the missing bond owners. They make the case that their records are more than thirty years old; people have moved or changed addresses, been married or divorced—so names change. The truth is that there are many reasons why they do not contact people who own bonds, and there are many reasons why bond owners do not realize they have this pot of money sitting there waiting for them.

The Bureau of Public Debt also makes the following statement:

> "In addition to lost, destroyed and forgotten savings bonds, each year thousands of new savings bonds and bond interest payments go undelivered when the savings bond owner moves and fails to provide a forwarding address. The US Treasury also has billions of dollars in outstanding bearer and registered securities (i.e., Treasury bonds and notes), as well as Postal Savings System Bonds and Postal Savings Notes (Freedom Shares)."

[www.unclaimedassets.com/US1.htm]

Every year, more than 25,000 bonds and bond interest payments go undelivered because of incorrect addresses. Odds are great that some of you reading this book are in that 25,000. Even more of you are part of the 55 million who own bonds.

Search Tips

If you ever want to research a topic like this, you can always start with Google. Type in US Savings Bonds. Always go to extensions with ".gov" in them first. They are the government web sites. You can use the aforementioned unclaimed assets web site and enter your information to find out if you are in the bond database. Some sites like this charge a small fee.

Always shop around for the site that doesn't charge a search fee. The web site www.savingsbonds.gov will take you to Treasury Direct; a free site. On this site, you will see three columns: One for individuals, one for institutions and one for government. The last topic listed for individuals is "Check Treasury Hunt to see if you own matured savings bonds." Give it a click. You will need to scroll down the page until you see "Start Search." Click there and enter your social security number.

You can enter your social security number or the SSN of another person who may have unredeemed bonds. Instantly, you will be told if there is anything in the system for that number… and there is no database search fee.

They tell you up front that the database is not perfect. What government database would be? They also tell you:

- ✔ Treasury Hunt does not contain a record of all savings bonds. This system only provides information on Series E bonds issued in 1974 and after.

- ✔ Treasury Hunt may not completely identify any/all savings bonds you may have lost… only those that have reached final maturity and were issued in 1974 and after.

- ✔ Savings bonds returned to the Treasury as undeliverable since 1996 can also be found by searching this system.

✔ Most records for registered Treasury notes and bonds can be searched through this system.

✔ Also, note that to file a claim for lost bonds, you must submit a Form PD F 1048, Claim for Lost, Stolen or Destroyed United States Savings Bonds. You will need to include information about dates of purchase, names on bonds and other pertinent information.

[www.savingsbonds.gov/indiv/tools/tools_treasuryhunt.htm]

Any forms you want are available for download, or they will mail them to you. They are very short and simple to fill out.

Always shop around for the site that does not charge a search fee.

I know of one gal who received a bond as a gift years ago with a $500 face value that she long forgot about. When she did the search and sent in the form, she received a check for $2,800. I hear great stories like this all the time.

This is a cool site to play around on. They offer savings bond calculators and wizards. With the turbulent economy, people are again looking for stable "sure things" and savings bonds fit that mold. If you want to see how savings bonds can add up and at what rate, punch in some numbers and let the calculators do their thing.

When you tire of this Free Money source, keep reading for even bigger and better news.

CHAPTER 7

Tax Refunds

The IRS has a huge giant massive big old pile of cash that isn't theirs. For example, they have unclaimed tax refunds to the tune of $1.1 billion from tax year 2007 alone. 2007 tax returns were due in 2008. The three year statute of limitations is 2011.

That means, April 15, 2011 has passed, and those folks who did not file a tax refund for 2007 (or earlier) lose claim to their refund. That money gets to go to the US Treasury. It does not go to you if you miss the statute deadline.

If you are due a refund, always file your tax return!

The flip side is that if you did file your 2007 tax return, the statute of limitations for them to audit you for that year has expired.

Lost Money

It seems wise to remind you about statutes. If you are expecting a tax refund, file the return timely. Get your money. Don't let Uncle Sam keep it.

I always want to encourage you to not use your tax return as a savings account. Sure, it's fun to get a refund, but you let the feds play with your money for a whole year and not pay you one cent of interest. Who really gets the better deal?

In the event you get a refund, don't let the check get lost. The number of missing refund checks is astounding.

Update your address when you move. If you receive a tax refund, have them deposit it directly into your bank account. This method is safer and the funds get put into your account quicker than if the IRS has to cut a check and send it "snail mail."

Pay attention to when you file, and if you don't get your refund within six weeks, follow up. Do not let your precious tax dollars fall through the cracks. If you do not receive your refund timely, contact the IRS. Go to www.irs.gov and click on "where's my refund?"

To research the missing refund, you need to know your social security number, your filing status (married filing jointly, single, married filing separately, head of household, or qualifying widow/er). You also need to know the dollar amount of the refund you are expecting. ALWAYS keep a copy of the return you filed.

You can update your address online. In the event you are owed a refund, you do want them to be able to find you. The IRS does not allow mail to be forwarded, so you want to be sure to stay up to date. There are more than 100,000 refund checks returned to the Internal Revenue Service each year.

I can't fathom it, but I've read that $500,000,000 in refund checks goes uncashed. Does that make any sense to you? If you lose the check, ask the IRS to issue another one. Don't let that money get away from you.

Watch out for scams. For several years, spammers claiming to be the IRS send out e-mails asking for information, including Social

Security numbers. Do not give out your SSN. The IRS will not contact you via e-mail to ask for sensitive information. Their web site is secure, but e-mails are not a good place to share private information.

> If you do not receive your refund timely, contact the IRS.

If you ever have a question about tax matters, you can call the toll-free customer service line at 800-829-1040. To call about your refund status, call the refund line at 800-829-1954. Again, have your social security number, filing status and refund amount ready.

For those of you who may not have filed tax returns and are due a refund, you won't pay a penalty for a late return. They cannot assess a penalty if there is no tax due. Remember: They can only give the refund if you file within the statute of limitations period, which is three years.

That means the 2011 tax return was due April 15, 2012 and you have until April 15, 2015 to get it filed to claim that refund. If you have unfiled refunds for years prior to that, you cannot get your money from the IRS unless you are reading this early in 2014.

You also know that if you have other years that you have not filed, the IRS can withhold your refund until you file those other returns.

Fear Not

I realize that the three little words Internal Revenue Service strike fear into the hearts of many. Filing a tax return does not have to be scary or complicated. There is help online from the IRS itself and many communities have volunteers who prepare tax returns as a free community service. Check with your local library or community service. Free tax return preparation is Free Money to you and gives added peace of mind. You can also file for free using free fill-in forms. Go to www.irs.gov and click on IRSe-file and freefile. Everyone can e-file, and everyone can e-file individual tax returns for free!

This chapter is really the tip of the iceberg when it comes to Free Money from the IRS. They actually give out Free Money, millions of dollars to millions of taxpayers. One of the best "inventions" ever is something called a tax credit.

There are so many tax credits, they deserve a chapter all their own.

CHAPTER 8

Tax Credits

No bull, no hype. The federal government has many Free Money programs and one of the best ever is from the Internal Revenue Service in the form of tax credits. Getting money from Uncle Sam with no strings and no payback is a beautiful thing.

There are MANY tax credits, but many folks don't know what they are. Want an extra $800 this year? File a Schedule M. Ever heard of it? Many people haven't. If you are a working person, you need to know. Don't worry. We'll get to it.

There are so many credits to talk about, we just need to dig right in.

Tax Credits = Free Money

Don't assume that you won't get a refund when you file your tax return. Never assume anything.

Even if you had no tax withheld, there are tax credits that you may be entitled to that will create money in your pocket… but you need to file a tax return in order to claim them.

The list of tax credits is amazing. Most people have no idea how many credits there really are. Here is a short list:

✔ Lifetime learning credit

✔ Child tax credit

✔ Earned income tax credit

✔ Credit for child and dependent care

✔ American Opportunity Credit

✔ Making Work Pay credit

You can jump onto www.irs.gov for the whole list. You can also do a Google search for tax credits in general or for a specific topic. Don't forget the free IRS 800 number, your local tax advisors and the free community help that is available.

Making Work Pay

I don't know who gets the job to name these credits. I suppose the straight forward "Making Work Pay" is better than the grandiose "American Opportunity" credit. That's a bit vague. And yes, we'll get to that one, too.

Many people overlook the Making Work Pay credit. It is a "bonus" given to working taxpayers. This credit is refundable, which is another beautiful word. A refundable credit means you will get that money refunded to you even if you owe no tax.

Some credits are applied against the tax amount and if the tax due gets reduced down to zero, then you are done. You owe nothing, but you get nothing back. These refundable credits can reduce the tax down to zero and the balance is refunded to you.

The Making Work Pay credit is $400 for single workers and $800 for those married filing joint. Even if you have zero tax, you will still get the $400 or the $800.

You are eligible for this credit if you received wages from a job or were self-employed. File the Schedule M to claim this credit. The instructions and the forms for all the credits are available at www.irs.gov where they can be download for free.

I am not a fan of everything our government does, and the American Recovery and Reinvestment Act of 2009 had its hits and misses. But creating a new way to take home an extra $800 of Free Money is a hit.

Child Credit

The child tax credit has been around a long time. It basically gives a boost to those raising a family and trying to make ends meet. The amount of the credit can be up to $1,000 per qualifying child.

> In a nutshell, you get a credit of $1,000 per child.

Nice.

But the instructions aren't nice. They don't make it simple. It's not all that complicated, but the wording isn't clear.

"You may be able to claim the child tax credit if you have a qualifying child."

The wise old owls at the IRS give this as their definition of a "qualifying child."

1. Is a United States citizen, resident or national;

2. Is under age 17 at the end of the calendar year;

3. Is your son, daughter, stepson, stepdaughter, legally adopted child, or a child placed with you for legal adoption, brother, sister, stepbrother, stepsister, foster child or a descendant of any such person; AND

4. Shares with you the same principal residence for more than one-half of the tax year, or is treated as your qualifying child under the special rule for parents who are divorced, separated or living apart.

Basically, for most of you, assuming you are a US citizen, if your child is still under age 17, you probably meet the requirements for "qualifying child."

For the in-depth nitty gritty on how to get $1,000 per child, get IRS Publication 672.

If you have one child, your credit is $1,000 (limited to income restrictions that will phase out the credit the more money you make. Married filing jointly, the income limit is $110,000; and single, it is $75,000).

If your tax due is $1,000, you apply the credit and that wipes out the tax. You owe nothing. If your tax bill is $1,400, you would only owe $400.

This credit is not refundable. That means if you owe $500 in tax and your credit is $1,000, you eliminate all tax, but you do not get an extra $500 refund.

To claim the credit, it is as easy as checking a box on the front of the return where you enter the names and social security numbers of your children.

If you have two kids, and can apply two grand against your tax bill, I think you should take the kiddies out for ice cream.

Additional Child Tax Credit

There is another credit, and this one is refundable. It's called the Additional Child Tax Credit and is intended to help working families. This credit kicks in if your income is below a low-income threshold. You can get a refund of the credit even if you don't owe any tax. If you qualify, fill out Form 8812 to get this money back to you. Think of it like a bonus prize from the government.

> You can get a refund of the credit even if you don't owe any tax.

Child and Dependent Care Credit

This credit is different from the child tax credit explained above. See what I mean about all kinds of Free Money tax credits! You can take the child tax credit and, if you pay day care expenses, you can also take the child care credit.

To claim this credit, you have to pay childcare expenses so you can work or look for work. Use IRS Publication 503 for all the information and instructions. You need to file Form 2441. The kids being cared for have to be under age 13.

There are income limits and rules as to how much expense you can use to compute your credit. The day care providers have to provide their social security numbers. Your credit is a percentage of the expense you pay. Depending upon your income, you can get a deduction of at least 20% and up to 35%. This form drives some people bonkers but, if you carefully follow the instructions on Form 2441, it walks you through the process of computing the credit without too much mumbo jumbo.

The credit varies from person to person because it's based on what you pay for child care and what your earned income is. For example, if you pay $3,000 for daycare and your income is over $43,000, you get 20% of the $3,000 as your credit. That's $600. Nice.

If you pay $6,000 for two kids to go to daycare while you work, and have income less than $15,000, your credit is 35% of the $6,000. That's a credit of $2,100. Even nicer! If I read the material correctly, the maximum credit you can take is $5,000. Five grand! Even nicer!

The only downside is that this credit is not refundable. It can wipe your tax down to zero, which means you pay nothing. That's good. But the extra is not refundable. Too bad. But child-based tax credits are a wonderful source of Free Money. This is one area of the federal government that gets no complaints from me.

Earned Income Credit

The Earned Income Tax Credit (EITC) is a refundable credit. Gotta love that. The key words here are earned income. That means a job… or earnings from self-employment.

If you have income that you earned from working, check into the requirements for this credit. And in case you were wondering, you don't have to have a child to qualify for this credit. You just have to have earned income.

The basic rules for this credit are:

- ✔ You must have a valid Social Security Number.
- ✔ You must have earned income from employment or from self-employment.
- ✔ Your filing status cannot be married filing separately.
- ✔ You must be a U.S. citizen or resident alien all year, or a nonresident alien married to a U.S. citizen or resident alien and filing a joint return.

✔ You cannot be a qualifying child of another person. If you do not have a qualifying child, you must:
- o be age 25 but under 65 at the end of the year,
- o live in the United States for more than half the year, and
- o not qualify as a dependent of another person.

The IRS is trying to make this credit easier to figure out. That laundry list above may not prove that point, but they are trying to simplify the process. You can go to the IRS web site to the EITC Assistant to help figure the credit.

Let's check income requirements.

2013 Tax Year (to be filed by April 15, 2014)

Earned Income and adjusted gross income (AGI) must each be less than:
- o $45,060 ($50,270 married filing jointly) with three or more qualifying children
- o $41,952 ($47,162 married filing jointly) with two qualifying children
- o $36,920 ($42,130 married filing jointly) with one qualifying child
- o $13,980 ($19,190 married filing jointly) with no qualifying children

Tax Year 2013 maximum credit:
- o $5,891 with three or more qualifying children
- o $5,236 with two qualifying children
- o $3,169 with one qualifying child
- o $475 with no qualifying children

And, last but not least, investment income must be $3,200 or less for the year

Let me repeat. It's a refundable credit. You could get $5,891 from the Internal Revenue Service. Tax credit? Gift? Either way it's Free Money!

Go to www.irs.gov to check the dollar amounts for each tax year, or if you have questions about this credit.

> **Many people are entitled to this EITC and do not claim it.**

You can see that you do not have to have a child for this credit, but if you do, you get more of a credit. Give that kid a hug.

Many people are entitled to the EITC and do not claim it. If you want to read more, get IRS Publication 596. If you qualify for the EITC, you may also be entitled to a similar credit on your state tax return.

For the list of states that offer EITC, check out: www.irs.gov/Individuals/States-and-Local-Governments-with-Earned-Income-Tax-Credit.

Visit www.irs.gov/Individuals/States-and-Local-Governments-with-Earned-Income-Tax-Credit for all the detailed info on the Earned Income Tax Credit.

Education Tax Credits

Education tax credits can help offset the costs of higher education for you or your children. Tuition is outrageous. If you can get any break, take it.

For some credits, you or your student needs to be enrolled full time. Read the nitty gritty or talk to a tax professional. Also, check online. The IRS web site is actually user friendly and chock full of info.

Form 8863 is what you need to file to claim the American Opportunity credit or the Lifetime Learning credit. You can take the American Opportunity credit for four years per student. You can't take the American Opportunity credit and the Lifetime Learning credit for the same student for the same year. You have to pick which is most beneficial to you at that time.

If you have more than one student in your household, it's possible to claim both of the credits.

The Lifetime Learning Credit applies to undergrad, graduate and professional level degrees. This credit is 20% of the first $10,000 you pay in tuition and fees, up to a maximum of $2,000 per year.

There are limits on the amount of income you may have to be able to claim the credit. Certain income ranges create a reduced credit.

Part of the credit may be refundable and part is nonrefundable. Don't ask me why they have to confuse the issue.

Also adding to the confusion is that credits come and go. The Hope Credit is now old news. The American Opportunity credit is now allowed. This credit allows up to a $2,500 credit on tuition expenses paid in a year… but it has income limits, too. It is available for the first four years of postsecondary education.

Read all the rules in the publication and instructions. For example, the student cannot have any felony drug convictions. I am puzzled how that caveat entered the rulebooks. If a student is now in college trying to better himself and the credit is indeed called the American Opportunity credit, it seems it should apply. But it doesn't.

It is what it is. But it can mean Free Money.

To get the full scoop, check out www.irs.gov or get Publication 970. In case I have not mentioned it, ALL forms and publications for all credits can be downloaded at www.irs.gov for free.

Qualified Retirement Savings Contributions

The purpose of this credit is to help workers save for retirement and get a tax break now. If you put money into an IRA (Individual Retirement Account) or your employer's 401(k) plan, this Saver's Credit may apply to you.

The credit can be claimed by:

✔ Married couples filing jointly with incomes up to $55,500;

✔ Heads of Household with incomes up to $41,625;

✔ Married individuals filing separately and singles with incomes up to $27,750.

The maximum Saver's Credit is $1,000 for single filers and $2,000 for married couples. I like that Free Money.

A taxpayer's credit amount is based on filing status, adjusted gross income, tax liability and the amount contributed to qualifying retirement programs. Form 8880 is used to claim the Saver's Credit, and the instructions have details on how to figure the credit.

Saver's Credits totaling almost $900 million have been claimed. Begun in 2002 as a temporary provision, the Saver's Credit was made a permanent part of the tax code in legislation enacted in 2006. The income limits have not changed during the past several years, but are subject to increase, which is a good thing, to keep up with inflation.

First Time Homebuyer Credit

As we go to press, the first time homebuyers' credit has expired. It was a huge boon to the housing market after the foreclosure fiasco and the market went stagnant. To get folks buying again, an $8,000 credit was given.

It was a huge success.

This credit may or may not surface again. The feds are always creating new programs, so home buyer credits may appear again.

> Ask your tax advisor to double check for any credits you may have missed.

Stay in tune with what is going on. Before you file your tax return, read the "What's New" section for the tax year to determine if there are new credits or programs that apply to you. Ask your tax advisor to double check for any credits you may have missed.

Think if you had been eligible for an $8,000 credit and missed it! That's a boatload of Free Money!

The deadline for home purchases was extended until September 30, 2010. If for some reason you qualify for this credit, or any credit, and failed to take it on your 2010 return, you can file an amended return. You can file an amended return up to three years past the April 15 due date of the original return.

Energy Credits

Green is big. Do green things to your home and Uncle Sam will send you some green for making the planet a nicer place.

It is, actually, a great deal. You make home improvements that save you money every month on your energy bills and you get a benefit back from the government. Some states and local governments give credits, rebates and refunds, too. Check with your state and community to see what deals are offered, or you can one-stop shop at this web site with the clever government name: dsireusa.org.

Their site explains: "DSIRE is a comprehensive source of information on state, local, utility and federal incentives and policies that promote renewable energy and energy efficiency. Established in 1995 and funded by the U.S. Department of Energy, DSIRE is an ongoing project of the N.C. Solar Center and the Interstate Renewable Energy Council."

Click on your state to get started. You find a bunch of financial incentives. Each state has a huge database for solar energy programs, rebates and other incentives. There is information there to keep you reading for years.

The site also gives related program info, which we have taken verbatim:

Alternative Fuels and Advanced Vehicles Data Center

The U.S. Department of Energy's Alternative Fuels and Advanced Vehicles Data Center (AFDC) provides a wide range of information and resources to enable the use of alternative fuels and other petroleum-reduction options, such as advanced vehicles, fuel blends, idle reduction and fuel economy. The AFDC site offers a database of state and federal laws and incentives related to alternative fuels and vehicles, air quality, fuel efficiency, and other transportation-related topics.

Green Power Network

The U.S. Department of Energy's Green Power Network provides news and information on green power markets and activities, including opportunities to buy green power. This site provides state-by-state information on green power marketing and utility green power programs. In addition, the site lists marketers of renewable energy credits (RECs), also known as green tags or renewable energy certificates, which represent the environmental attributes of the power produced from renewable energy projects.

Weatherization Assistance Program

The U.S. Department of Energy's Weatherization Assistance Program (WAP) enables low-income families to reduce their energy bills by making their homes more energy-efficient. Through this program, weatherization service providers install energy-efficiency measures in the homes of qualifying homeowners free of charge. The WAP program web site offers a state-by-state map of opportunities, projects and activities.

Wind Powering America

The U.S. Department of Energy's Wind Powering America site provides state-by-state information on wind projects and activities, including wind working groups, validated wind maps, anemometer loan programs, small wind guides, state-specific news, wind for schools, workshops and web casts.

Green, Green, Green

As you may have realized by now, the options are many. Buying a green car, for example, can reap big cash back in your pocket from multiple sources. You can do things around the house, too. If you are not sure where to start, have a home energy audit. An audit is an inspection that can determine where you are wasting energy and what you can do about it. Insulation, doors, windows and appliances all are potential energy leaks.

It's a good idea to have your furnace and air conditioner checked out once a year to make sure they are operating safely and efficiently. The energy audit is an additional step you can take to find ways to save on your utility bills. Go to www.resnet.us/home-energy-audits to find additional ways to improve energy efficiency in your home.

Upgrading doors and windows and getting a programmable thermostat are all ways to get a kick back. Buying a new water heater could qualify for a tax credit. Check out www.doe.gov and www.energystar.gov for more info.

Their web site shows you how easy it is to reduce energy use at home and on the road. The easy, practical solutions for saving energy include tips you can use today, throughout your home… from the roof, walls and insulation that enclose it to the appliances and lights inside.

> The energy audit is an additional step you can take to find ways to save on your utility bills.

The energystar.gov site also has a page that contains links to current tax credits that may apply to your situation. Very handy.

Ever heard of power vampires? You might not have heard the term, but I bet you figured out the meaning… things that keep sucking power.

Back in the day, the only command used to be, "Turn off the lights when you leave a room." Now you have to check to see if all your gizmos and gadgets are turned off and all chargers are unplugged. Even when electronics are turned off, they are still sucking power. 25% of electricity is used when these things are actually turned off.

Think about the expanse of electronic things we have now. Think about how much we leave plugged in, either turned on or turned off. Think of how much more electricity we use now in this modern era.

Of all the countries on this planet, the United States consumes 25% of the world's energy. About 5% of that is vampire power. When you equate that to the bigger picture, our wasted energy is the amount of power that the entire country of Italy uses in a year.

It makes sense, and cents, for the US to want to do something about our use of energy. Giving credits to encourage better consumer use of resources is a pretty good idea. To make things easy on you, start simple. If you're not using it, unplug it. Use a power strip so all you have to do is flip one switch to turn off several things at once.

As we go to press, most of the credits are available through 2016, so you still have time to update your home and nab a good Free Money credit, too.

Audits

FYI—Word is out the IRS is going to increase the number of its mail audits. What that means is the feds will send you a letter questioning something on your tax return and you have to send back proof of that deduction.

If you get such a notice, double-check their math, your math and the form calculation. Sometimes the Internal Revenue Service is wrong.

Keep your records in a file with your copy of your tax return so that if you are questioned, you have the documentation handy. Saved time means saved money.

As you progress through this tax year, keep your receipts and records as you go. Keep a file folder to keep track of paperwork. It will save tons of time at tax prep time next year and you will thank yourself for doing yourself this favor.

Don't freak out if you get an audit notice. There is always the chance that any correction to your return will result in a refund. Many people actually pay in too much.

If you get a letter from the IRS, a CP 2000 letter, stating that they have "corrected" your return and now you owe more, you can fight it. And, you can get FREE help to do it. Visit www.irs.gov/advocate to contact your local taxpayer advocate. This person will provide advice and representation for FREE. Free tax help equals Free Money.

Free Tax Help

The IRS trains volunteers to file returns for folks for free.

Google free tax advice in your area. In Chicago there is a nonprofit organization called Ladder Up. Started in Chicago in 1994 by an accountant who still is the head of the agency, Ladder Up educates people on how to claim all the credits they are due and helps prepare their returns.

Normally, it costs about $150 to get a tax return prepared by a tax professional. Many folks just can't afford it. That is the first savings that Ladder Up provides, no charge for tax help. That's an extra $150 in Free Money for the people they serve.

This group of 16,000 volunteers has returned over $335 million to 165,000 families. Ladder Up partners with local community agencies like the YMCA, churches and schools. The volunteers who prepare the returns are trained to maximize the tax credits available to these folks. One gal discovered that she was owed $10,000 by the IRS!

Go to www.goladderup.org if you are in the Chicago area. Additionally, many other communities offer free help. There are local organizations and schools that offer free tax services. Call your community center and local libraries for dates and times. Also, the government itself has a great program for helping file tax returns. The IRS trains volunteers to file returns for folks for free.

Get the scoop on the Internal Revenue Service's Volunteer Income Tax Assistance program (VITA) and the Tax Counseling for the Elderly (TCE) programs that offer free tax help for taxpayers who qualify at their web site: http://www.irs.gov/Individuals/Free-Tax-Return-Preparation-for-You-by-Volunteers.

In addition to the free tax preparations, VITA and TCE programs, there is more. The feds also offer help for the military via the Armed Forces Tax Council. These folks are trained to help our military personnel with their specific tax issues.

If you are Army, Navy, Air Force, Marines or Coast Guard, go to www.militaryonesource.mil/ to get free tax prep help. This site also hooks you up with free help from a local H&R Block office if you want to prepare your own return. (Yes, some people do that.) For any questions, Military One Source has a free tax helpline at 800-342-9647.

The AARP also offers tax help for seniors, so you have that option, if you are over age fifty. Their web site is www.aarp.org/money/taxes/aarp_taxaide/ or call 877-434-7598.

In addition to return preparation, many people have questions or need help dealing with the IRS regarding old problems or new questions. There is free or low-cost assistance for these problems, too.

The IRS offers Taxpayer Assistance Centers (TAC) all over the country. They help with return filing, payment plans or how to understand a letter you receive from the IRS. If you do not want to deal with waiting on the 800 phone line or do not want to go back and forth in the mail, you can talk with someone face to face at a Taxpayer Assistance Center. To find one close to you, visit www.irs.gov, click on Help & Resources, then click contact my local office and then enter your ZIP code.

If you need help to resolve tax problems and have been unable to do so by dealing directly with the IRS, you can use the Taxpayer Advocate. This is an independent organization from the IRS and reports directly to Congress. The Taxpayer Advocate Service can be very helpful in resolving problems. You can call them toll-free at 877-777-4778.

Another option: Low-Income Tax Clinics provide free or low-cost assistance to taxpayers who need help to resolve their tax problems. If you have an income tax audit or a collection dispute, these Tax Clinics can provide you with legal representation if you need to go to Tax Court to resolve your problems.

Tax Clinics also provide assistance to people whose primary language is other than English. Local non-profits, universities and law schools operate these Tax Clinics. They receive some funding from the IRS and are supervised by the National Taxpayer Advocate. Visit www.irs.gov/advocate to find a directory of these tax clinics.

If you are in the mood to peruse the web for all things tax related (dreary rainy day perhaps?), asktaxguru.com is a great site to get general tax info and advice. What, you may ask, can you do at asktaxguru? Their response: "AskTaxGuru is a free online US tax resource and support community, with helpful features such as Local Tax Professional Search, Tax Tips, Tax Calculators, Free Downloads and Resources."

And remember, an audit or a letter from the IRS is really no big deal. Do not panic. There is plenty of help out there for you and, when all is said and done, it very well could end up meaning Free Money for you… a little something called a refund.

IRS on YouTube

It's the phenomenon of the modern world. If you need to know how to tie a tie, dye Easter eggs or take a tax credit, it's on YouTube.

Everything is on YouTube. Even the IRS.

Uncle Sam and the Internal Revenue Service have their own YouTube Channel. They have a bunch of videos offering tips on many topics, from "Where is my Refund?" to "Free File" to how to use their web site.

I poke fun, but it's actually brilliant for the IRS to join the online community. Video tutorials are helpful and offering assistance for free is a great benefit to all American taxpayers. Free tax help is Free Money.

If you want to see for yourself, go to YouTube and type IRS in the search field.

I don't see any singing or comedy, and it's not as entertaining as most YouTube videos, but the fact that the IRS has a web presence is smart. Some of the videos are very short and simple. The IRS posts their scripts on their web site:

> "Hi. My name is Eric and I work for the Internal Revenue Service.
>
> Do you make non-cash contributions to charity? If you do, you can join the millions of Americans who, every year, donate to qualified charitable organizations and, as a result, save on their taxes.
>
> Normally, if you give used clothing or other household items to charity those items must be in good used condition or better. As a general rule, that's the only way you'll get a tax deduction for the items that you donate. Your deduction is based on the fair market value of the items that you donate. Well, "what in the world is that," you say? Well, basically, the fair market value is the amount that a willing buyer would pay to a willing seller for that item. And, most of the time that's a lot less than the original retail price of that item.
>
> Keeping good records is always of good idea; so, be sure to ask the charity for a receipt and be sure to keep a list of the items that you donate. And, one final point to keep in mind: to get a tax benefit from items that you donate, you must itemize your deduction on Schedule A.
>
> To find out more about charitable contributions go to the IRS web site and download Publication 526. So you don't forget, do it today. Download it from our very

popular web site www.IRS.gov."

We'll give the IRS a thumbs up for that.

Believe it or not, the IRS also has a Facebook page. You can find IRS forms and publications, hot topics, tools, news, filing and payments, refunds, credits and deductions, help and other resources.

We like that!

Obama Administration

The last go-round of this book was the advent of the Obama administration and the promise of "change." The creation of the American Recovery and Reinvestment Act is amusing in retrospect. Read what the bombasters wrote about their act when it first came to be:

"The American Recovery and Reinvestment Act is an unprecedented effort to jumpstart our economy, create or save millions of jobs, and put a down payment on addressing long-neglected challenges so our country can thrive in the 21st century. The Recovery and Reinvestment Act 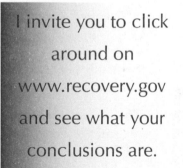 is an extraordinary response to a crisis unlike any since the Great Depression. With much at stake, the Act provides for unprecedented levels of transparency and accountability so that you will be able to know how, when, and where your tax dollars are being spent. Spearheaded by a new Recovery Board, this Act contains built-in measures to root out waste, inefficiency, and unnecessary spending. This web site, recovery.gov, will be the main vehicle

I invite you to click around on www.recovery.gov and see what your conclusions are.

to provide each and every citizen with the ability to monitor the progress of the recovery." [Source: www.recovery.gov]

I thought I'd check up on their "unprecedented levels of transparency and accountability" and see how we are doing now.

There are graphics and charts scattered about.

They claim $290.7 billion of tax benefits.

For federal grants, a chart shows funds awarded of nearly $247 billion and entitlements at about $238 billion.

So far, my ability to monitor progress is a bit muddled.

The government has a Flickr account with a slideshow of various "recovery projects." I haven't come across any Spring Break pics, yet.

I clicked on the tab up top labeled "Where is the money going?" You can enter your Zip code to see projects in your neighborhood, view agency summary information or search by recipient.

I invite you to click around on www.recovery.gov and see what your conclusions are. The site, "US Government's official web site that provides easy access to data related to Recovery Act spending" also wants you to be their Facebook friend.

"Hey, friend me" are words I never thought I'd hear from a US government official web site.

So, I guess in some respects, the Obama administration has indeed brought about change.

State Tax Credits

Don't forget there are also STATE tax credits! This is just one example and one state, but take a gander at Illinois Form 1299-D to see the list of state tax credits available to businesses:

- ✔ TECH-PREP Youth Vocational Programs Credit
- ✔ Dependent Care Assistance Program Credit
- ✔ Film Production Services Tax Credit
- ✔ Employee Child Care Tax Credit (Form IL-1120 filers only)
- ✔ Jobs Tax Credit • Enterprise Zone Investment Credit
- ✔ River Edge Redevelopment Zone Investment Credit
- ✔ High Impact Business Investment Credit
- ✔ Tax Credit for Affordable Housing Donations
- ✔ Economic Development for a Growing Economy (EDGE) Credit
- ✔ Research and Development Tax Credit
- ✔ River Edge Redevelopment Zone Remediation Credit
- ✔ Ex-Felons Jobs Credit
- ✔ Veterans Jobs Credit
- ✔ Student-Assistance Contribution Credit
- ✔ Angel Investment Credit
- ✔ New Markets Credit
- ✔ River Edge Historic Preservation Credit (short-year filers only)
- ✔ Live Theater Production Credit (short-year filers only)
- ✔ Historical Preservation Credit

There are also credits to take on your Illinois individual tax return—property tax credit, education expense credit and earned income tax credit.

No matter which state you live in, there will be tax credits. To determine what is applicable to you, consult your tax advisor or contact your state office. Web sites and contact information for each state are listed in Appendix 1.

CHAPTER 9

Pensions

Another Free Money source waiting for you to claim is lost pensions. There is a huge jackpot of unclaimed pension benefits sitting there waiting to go to the rightful owners. Think about it. You, or your parents, worked long and hard for many years, and deserve that company pension.

Companies come and go. They change hands, names and owners numerous times, and pension plans can get terminated when a new owner takes over. The people due their money don't always get it.

You might also leave behind a small pension when you change jobs. Who knows all the reasons why it happens; it just happens. People have lost money. That's Free Money sitting in an old pension account.

PBGC

The Pension Benefit Guaranty Corporation (PBGC) is the government agency that is the caretaker of pensions. In their hands are millions and millions of dollars in unclaimed pension benefits.

The PBGC states that benefits range from a buck to over $600,000! The average per person payout is roughly $5,000. A press release from July 2010 states that they are holding almost $197 million in unclaimed pension benefits.

The states with the most missing pension recipients and pension funds are New York, California, New Jersey, Texas, Ohio, Pennsylvania and Illinois. If you live in any of those states or worked in any of those states, you need to perk up. And no matter what state you live or work in, you need to check and see if you have unclaimed pension benefits that belong to you.

The PBGC has set up an online search directory similar to the ones we talked about earlier. Go to www.pbgc.gov to see if you or someone you know is owed a pension. Search by your last name, company name and the state where the company was headquartered.

> A press release from July 2010 states that they are holding almost $197 million in unclaimed pension benefits.

There is another bit of advice on their web site. People who believe that a pension plan owes them a benefit and they may be missing from the plan records should first try to contact the pension plan administrator or the company where they earned their pension. If the company cannot be found, they can contact PBGC by e-mailing missing@pbgc.gov or by writing to the PBGC Pension Search Program, 1200 K Street NW, Washington, D.C. 20005-4026.

The person should provide name, address, daytime telephone number, Social Security number, date of birth, the name and location of the employer and, if possible, the dates of employment, the name of the pension plan, the nine-digit Employer Identification Number (EIN) and the three-digit Plan Number (PN).

Lost and Found

They have an entire booklet online on how to find a lost pension. For a load of helpful information, visit the following web address and download the booklet for free: http://www.pbgc.gov/Documents/Finding_A_Lost_Pension.pdf

Over the past few years, more than 22,000 people have found $137 million in unclaimed pension benefits through this search tool! That is worth a minute of your time!

To avoid getting lost in the future, make sure you tell your employer when you move or change names. And, with the ever-changing structure of corporate America, you need to keep track of when your company moves or changes names. Any pension information you receive should be filed away safely so you know where to collect your benefits when the time comes.

A minute's worth of record keeping and organization is worth a lifetime of working for that pension.

You can also contact the PBGC at www.pbgc.gov if you are searching for pension benefits for a deceased family member. If you are a beneficiary, you may be able to collect the benefits.

Of course, you could try it the old-fashioned way and contact the employer directly. That can be a good first place to start, if you think you have money in a past pension plan. Contact the company or the plan administrator. That is the person(s) or entity that is/are ultimately responsible for the oversight, management and administration of the pension plan, and the administration and investment of the pension fund.

Now that you know, if you have a pension, stay up to date. Keep a record of the name of the plan, the dates that you worked

KEVIN TRUDEAU'S FREE MONEY

there and, if you're really on the ball, write down the plan number and the employer identification number of your company. This information should be on a statement or on your paperwork when you enrolled in the pension plan.

A little effort now to keep things in order will mean money in your pocket down the road. Keep that money in your pocket… where it belongs.

CHAPTER 10

Benefits

The sources for free money are endless. Is that evident by now? Let me do a quick study of some more.

Life Insurance

It's hard enough to lose a loved one. That loved one had a life insurance policy for you, a family member. Your relative paid the premiums all those years and the benefits are not going to where he or she intended—you. It's a doubly sad thing that many life insurance policy benefits go unclaimed.

It's not wrong or greedy to pursue finding life insurance benefits. That money is sitting waiting to be collected by the beneficiaries.

They are entitled to it, plain and simple.

Sometimes employers give life insurance policies through payroll deduction. Sometimes banks will give small policies to their account holders. And, of course, there are policies that a person buys through a major life insurance company.

When there is a death, the family members have to report it to the life insurance company in order to collect policy benefits, but if they do not know a policy exists, the company cannot issue the money.

Also in recent years, some of the major life insurance companies have changed the way they are structured. In something called demutualization, they converted to stock ownership, which simply means that policyholders and their beneficiaries are entitled to receive stock and cash, plus the insurance benefits.

Companies like Met Life, Prudential and John Hancock made this conversion. And, when the switch occurred, the records were discovered to need updating.

John Hancock did not have accurate addresses for 400,000 policyholders.

Met Life had 60 million shares unclaimed.

Prudential had 1.2 million policyholders that they could not locate.

It happens all the time. People move and the forwarding order for the post office expires. People marry and divorce and change names. People die.

Billions

In a single year, unclaimed life insurance benefits can be more than $20 billion. The average amount claimed by heirs or owners of the policies is only about $1 billion. That means there are billions still unclaimed.

To find abandoned life insurance funds:

✔ Perform a search of the unclaimed property databases in each state that you or your loved one lived in and worked in. (See Appendix)

✔ Search the National Unclaimed Property Network, which has a link for life insurance companies to search them directly.

(http://nupn.com/insurancecompanylist.htm) Hundreds of insurance companies are listed by name with address and phone number provided.

✔ Visit NAUPA, the National Association for Unclaimed Property Administrators—www.unclaimed.org.

✔ Visit www.missingmoney.org.

✔ Be a detective. What do I mean by that? If you are wondering about a deceased loved one's insurance benefits, you can be smart and track down some clues on your own.

   o Search bank books and checking accounts for payments made to life insurance companies.

   o Search their records for anything at all that is insurance related.

   o Contact the insurance agent who carried their house or car policies. They may also have life insurance policies on your family member.

   o Contact the financial advisor. He or she may be aware of any life insurance policies.

   o Contact the accountant or attorney of your loved one. They may be aware of policies and other items.

   o Contact current and former employers.

   o Look at the prior tax returns to see if there is any interest related to life insurance.

   o Watch the mail in the year following the death. There may be premium notices or other mailings from insurance companies.

   o Check state unclaimed property offices.

o If there is any possibility that life insurance may have been purchased in Canada, you can contact the Canadian Life and Health Insurance Association via phone 800-268-8099 to reach consumer assistance or visit www.clhia.ca.

o Contact the National Association of Insurance Commissioners (NAIC) Life Insurance Company Location System. The main site is www.naic.org.

> **In a single year, unclaimed life insurance benefits can be over $20 billion.**

Remember, when searching for lost funds, be it life insurance or bank accounts or whatever, keep in mind that money could be held in several states, not just the last address. If you—or your loved one—worked or lived anywhere, even for a short time, there may be money in those unclaimed offices. It is worth the search time when you uncover assets. Some states report the average disbursement is $1,000.

If you have $1,000 or several thousand out there, you will be glad that you took a few extra minutes to search all possible states.

Veterans Benefits

Maybe your loved one was a veteran. Benefits may have been lost in the record keeping process of the Department of Veterans Affairs. Same story, people move, people change names and people die.

For all the info on veterans' benefits, visit www.va.gov. The toll free telephone number for beneficiaries for veterans' pension benefits is 877-294-6380. The main line is 877-827-1000. For questions on service members and/or the Veterans Group Life Insurance Program, call 1-800-419-1473. For all other VA life insurance programs, call 1-800-669-8477.

The usual "found money" items for veterans' benefits are life insurance, burial allowances and disability payments. Members of the armed forces, and their heirs, may be entitled to Adjusted Service Bonds (ASB) which were issued in registered form to World War I veterans, and Armed Forces Leave Bonds (AFLB), issued in registered form to World War II veterans as compensation for accumulated but unused leave.

If you have an issue with military pay that you believe was never received, the Defense Finance and Accounting Service handles that.

The personnel records are maintained in the National Personnel Records Center/Military Personnel Records office (NPRC-MPR). A form DD-214 is required to process most claims, including those for burial assistance, life insurance and pensions. You can get this form via the internet at www.archives.gov.

Service members or beneficiaries who believe they may be entitled to unclaimed insurance should contact:

> Office of Service Members Group Life Insurance (OSGLI)
> 80 Livingston Avenue
> Roseland, New Jersey 07068-1733
> (800) 419-1473

To search the Veterans Unclaimed Insurance Funds database, go to: www.benefits.va.gov/insurance/.

Funds could include death awards, dividend checks and premium refunds owed to missing, current and former policyholders or beneficiaries. These benefits could arise from United States Government Life Insurance, National Service Life Insurance, Veterans Special Life Insurance, Veterans Reopened Insurance and Service-Disabled Veterans Life programs (not SGLI or VGLI).

(Source: www.unclaimed.com/va_benefit.htm)

Veterans Tax Credit

If you're an employer, there's another way you can get FREE MONEY and do something consequential at the same time. You can earn income tax credits for your company by hiring veterans, or you can receive salary reimbursements for hiring a veteran.

The Work Opportunity Tax Credit (WOTC) is a Federal tax credit available to private-sector businesses and certain non-profit organizations for hiring certain individuals, including veterans, who've consistently faced significant barriers to employment.

The Work Opportunity Tax Credit can now be as much as: $2,400 generally for each new adult hire, $1,200 for each summer youth hire, $4,800 for each new disabled veteran hire, and $9,000 for each new long-term Temporary Assistance for Needy Families (TANF) recipient hired over a 2-yr. period.

Here's how the Work Opportunity Tax Credit works:

✔ For most groups, the WOTC is based on qualified wages paid to the employee during the first year of employment. The credit is generally capped at $6,000. The credit is 40% for those employed 400 hours or more (25% of qualified first-year wages for those employed at least 120 hours, but fewer than 400 hours).

✔ Summer youth employees—Wages are capped at $3,000 for 16- and 17-year-olds working for a 90-day period between May 1 and September 15.

✔ Disabled veterans—Wages are capped at $12,000.

✔ Long-term TANF recipients—Wages are capped at $10,000. The WOTC is also available for the employee's qualified second-year wages, also capped at $10,000. For this group, the credit is 40% of qualified first-year wages and 50% of qualified wages for the second year of employment.

To learn more about the WOTC, call your State WOTC Coordinator, visit the WOTC web site, http://www.doleta.gov/business/Incentives/opptax or call your local employment or state workforce agency. The telephone numbers of the State WOTC Coordinators are as follows:

Alabama—334-353-8037
Alaska—907-465-5955
Arizona—602-495-1861, Ext. 1002
Arkansas—501-682-3749
California—916-654-5857
California—866-593-0173 (Toll Free)
Colorado—303-318-8829
Connecticut—860-263-6066
Delaware—302-761-8121
District of Columbia—202-698-3540
Florida—850-921-3299
Georgia—404-656-3157
Hawaii—808-586-8819
Idaho—208-332-3570, Ext.-3318
Illinois—312-793-6811, Ext.-231
Indiana—317-232-7746
Iowa—515-281-9010
Kansas—785-296-7435
Kentucky—502-564-7456
Louisiana—225-342-2923
Maine—207-624-6390
Maryland—410-767-2080
Massachusetts—617-626-5730
Michigan—313-456-3363

Minnesota—651-259-7507

Mississippi—601-321-6084

Missouri—573-522-9581

Montana—406-444-9046

Nebraska—402-471-2693

Nevada—775-684-0321

New Hampshire—603-228-4079

New Jersey—609-292-8112

New Mexico—505-841-8501

New York—518-457-6823

North Carolina—919-733-4896

North Dakota—701-328-2997

Ohio—614-644-0966

Oklahoma—405-557-5371

Oregon—503-947-1672

Pennsylvania—717-783-3676

Puerto Rico—787-993-9400, Ext.-2315

Rhode Island—401-462-8724

South Carolina—803-737-2592

South Dakota—605-626-2302

Tennessee—615-253-6664

Texas—512-463-9926

Utah—801-526-9480

Vermont—802-828-4350

Virginia—804-786-5277

Virgin Islands—340-776-3700, Ext.-2055

Washington—360-407-5107

West Virginia—304-558-3452

Wisconsin—608-267-4442

Wyoming—307-235-3611

Special Employer Incentives (SEI) Program

If you're interested in hiring veterans who face extraordinary obstacles to obtaining employment, check out the Special Employer Incentives (SEI) program. It's for veterans who are hired by participating employers at the onset of the SEI program, and employment is expected to continue following successful completion of the SEI program. As a result, the SEI program benefits both employers and veterans.

Employers can receive reimbursement of up to 50% of the veteran's salary during the SEI program. It may cover:

✔ Additional educational expenses
✔ Loss of production
✔ Additional supplies and equipment

Not only will you get a qualified veteran trained to your needs and specifications, the VA provides the necessary tools, equipment, uniforms and other supplies. They may even help you make appropriate accommodations based on the individual needs of your new employee. To keep it easy, paperwork is kept to a minimum, and you receive VA support during training and placement follow-up phase to help with work or training related needs.

To contact a Vocational Rehabilitation and Employment representative, Call 1-800-827-1000 and you'll be connected to a point of contact at the Vocational Rehabilitation Division.

(Source: http://benefits.va.gov/vow/)

Social Security Benefits

Yet another area of unclaimed bucks is Social Security. Every year about a half-billion dollars in Social Security benefit checks are not cashed.

Re-read that last sentence.

> You need to know the social security number of anyone you want to search for lost benefits.

The Social Security Administration sends out the checks and if they go uncashed or unclaimed, that money just sits. The Social Security office is not beating the bushes looking for all the people to whom they owe money.

Before you begin searching for lost benefits, you'll need to know the social security number of that person or family member. You may be eligible for unclaimed benefits, if you are a beneficiary of a deceased loved one.

The Social Security Death Index (SSDI) has a record of reported deaths. This database maintains the social security number, date of birth, date of death, last known address and payment of final benefit.

Contact the Social Security Administration office in your town or online at their web site, www.ssa.gov.

To find a local office, go to https://secure.ssa.gov/ICON/main. jsp and enter your ZIP code.

Unclaimed Stock

Another benefit that goes missing is stock. The Securities and Exchange Commission (SEC) estimates there are three million lost stockholders who are entitled to unclaimed stock worth $10 BILLION!

Plus, there's another $500 million of bond interest and stock dividends not cashed each year.

Companies merge and restructure all the time now. The constant change means a lot of information gets lost in the shuffle. Companies acquire and sell off companies nearly every day. It is hard to keep up. If you had stock in Company X, you may now be eligible to receive shares of Company X, Company Y, and Company Z.

Let your fingers do the walking in the online database searches.

IRAs

There are also retirement accounts that have unclaimed money. About 50 million people have Individual Retirement Accounts (IRAs). At age 70 1/2 you have to start taking withdrawals from the IRA. Some such withdrawals are unclaimed or considered abandoned.

Every year about $850 million goes unclaimed.

Many people also have retirement funds in their employer's plans—401(k) plans. Every year about $850 million goes unclaimed. The usual reason for this missing money is that the company—the employer—has gone bankrupt or gone out of business. The money is left with the plan administrator and goes unclaimed by the rightful owners.

Who are the rightful owners? You!

Don't let another year go by without you getting what is rightfully yours. Do the search!

Gift Cards

Another item that people seldom think about are gift cards. Yep. You get them as gifts and lose them or forget about them. Gift cards are big business, especially during the holiday season. Don't know what to buy someone? Give them a gift card.

We've all done it.

More than $70 billion is spent on gift cards and gift certificates. For whatever reason, many do not get redeemed. It's estimated that close to ten percent are never cashed in. That could be up to $7 billion.

It varies state to state, but gift cards now are considered unclaimed property like all the other assets we have been discussing. Even though the actual gift card may have been lost, destroyed, or even expired, the value still exists and a refund may be entitled.

Some gift cards are even part of the unclaimed asset search system. And what a search system it is. My buddy Paul found $273 owed to him by Bed, Bath & Beyond within seconds!

Mining for Gold

Has the light bulb clicked? Do you see all the potential out there?

The database at missingmoney.com maintained by the National Association of Unclaimed Property Administrators (NAUPA) is a veritable gold mine. There are more possibilities for free money than I have fingers and toes. And all I need are my fingers to do the search. Same goes for National Unclaimed Property Network at http://nupn.com/. What are you waiting for?

Start panning for your gold!

CHAPTER 11

Inheritances & Gifts

There have been times I have heard someone say something like, "I wish I had a rich old uncle." They are not referring to Uncle Sam. They are wishing for some old rich uncle so that they can get some money via inheritance when the uncle moves on to greener pastures.

Hoping for Free Money to come to you in your time of economic hardship isn't as crazy as you may have thought. There are unclaimed inheritances and who knows, you could wind up with a windfall beyond your wildest dreams.

Everyone wishes for an inheritance because it is Free Money, usually a big fat sum… and if it's less than $1,500,000… you don't have to pay taxes on it. You also didn't have to do anything for it. It's a gift.

Actually, gifts are another source of Free Money that I forgot to mention thus far.

Gifts

Before we launch into the fertile field of inheritances, let's talk about gifts. You can receive a gift, tax free to you and to the person gifting you. This is a great way for your parents or grandparents or other relatives to share their wealth, reduce their possible future estate taxes, and be able to see their loved ones enjoy the "inheritance money" in the here and now.

> The person giving the gift usually does not have to worry about taxes until the gifts reach a maximum amount imposed by the IRS.

A gift does not typically get included on your tax return. If you receive a monetary gift under $13,000, you get the money tax free. Yippee!

The person giving you the money does not have to pay income taxes either. Usually. They don't get a deduction on their tax return; it is not an expense, it is merely a gift. It will reduce the size of their estate when they die, so reducing the amount of assets will reduce the possibility of having to pay estate taxes later on.

The person giving the gift usually does not have to worry about taxes until the gifts reach a maximum amount imposed by the IRS. FYI… A person can give their spouse unlimited gifts and there are no tax implications. If a donor gives another individual gifts that exceed a set amount during any year, there could be a gift tax imposed on the person giving the gift. It's still Free Money to you.

Here's some official info on this from the IRS web site: "Who pays the gift tax?

The donor is generally responsible for paying the gift tax. Under special arrangements the donee may agree to pay the tax instead. Please visit with your tax professional if you are considering this type of arrangement."

The current amount limit is $13,000. If the person is giving you money to pay education or medical bills, they do not have to pay gift tax, no matter how much they give. They can give you $13,000 as a no-strings gift AND pay your college education.

The $13,000 limit is per recipient. Let's say your father is wealthy and has ten kids. He can gift each child, no matter how old, $13,000, each year. There is no tax consequence to anyone… kids or dad.

You can check with the Internal Revenue Service or go to www.irs.gov for more information. There are lifetime limits to how much Big Daddy can gift before any tax issue kicks in. The only reason there is a gift tax is to prevent people from giving it all away before they die to avoid estate taxes. Don't get me going on that issue.

The good news is that you or any donor can gift a lifetime maximum of $5 million (just went up from $1 million) before you have to worry about gift taxes. The recipients of the gifts do not have to pay taxes on the gift ever. So if you have a wealthy relative or friend, clue them in that gifting is a great way to go. You could actually be helping them in their tax planning by allowing them to give you the gift of Free Money.

I love gifts. I love Free Money. I love the gift of Free Money.

Inheritances

Like I said, we all hold out a secret hope for a wad of cash appearing out of nowhere. We all want money with no strings. How many people do you know start out their wish list with statements like, "When I win the lottery...?" It's not the lottery that's compelling; it's the idea of a lump sum of cash that magically appears.

But let me get back to what I was talking about… a pot of gold at the end of the rainbow. People don't believe in leprechauns, but money comes from unlikely sources all the time.

There are people just like you who never in a million years dreamed that they would receive an inheritance. But it happens. And, many people are surprised when the money comes to them out of the blue.

Surprise

Money does indeed come out of the blue. The stuff I talk about in my books is real life stuff. In fact, there are two real life professionals who had a television show and they go around like fairy godmothers dropping inheritances and cash into people's laps.

John Hilbert and Shar Mansukhani have a great gig. Maybe you are familiar with Wealth Hunters or Heir Hunters International from television. In a nutshell, they track down people who have inheritances due them. They also reunite families sometimes in the process. Pretty impressive!

John believes many people in America have assets that are due them. Most people don't know it and until I started writing books like this, I didn't know the whole of it either, as the information was kept pretty secret.

Not anymore.

Shar says it could be an inheritance, it could be property rights, it could be the right to open a safety deposit box, but the reality is that most people don't know it's out there. They, Shar and John, have been working with state governments to reunite people with their lost money for the past two decades.

According to John, there are literally billions of dollars that have ended up in the hands of the government, just waiting to be claimed, but people just don't know how to get it. John and Shar enjoy being part of the process. They love seeing the look on peoples' faces when they tell them the news.

> They also come across inheritance information regarding others while researching their cases.

Every story has its own twists and turns along the way. It could be $200,000 to someone in Florida; it could be a million greenbacks to someone in Arizona.

John is a private investigator, and in a way, I am an investigator who makes my findings very public. What they do out of their office in LA, I tell people how to do in my books. John, Shar and I have this in common: we like research and we like to help people.

We know that there are inheritances and other sources of money going unclaimed that no one is talking about. The American public needs to know. Not everyone gets to be on TV, nor does everyone want to be on TV, but everyone does want to know if they have a lost inheritance out there. I certainly would. Wouldn't you?

To get information on John and Shar's work, you can contact them at http://heirhuntersinternational.info/, and the old fashioned way at:

Heir Hunters International
11755 Wilshire Blvd. 15th Floor
Los Angeles, California 90025

Toll Free: (888) 717-HEIR (4347)
Office: (310) 347-HEIR (6666)
Fax: (888) 717-4347
Email: johnhilbert@att.net

Part of what they do is take calls from people who are looking for a missing heir and subsequent inheritance. They also come across inheritance information regarding others while researching their cases. They then contact that person and proceed with the investigation to uncover who is due what. It's just like a treasure hunt.

If John or Shar or their company contacts you, odds are they found money for you.

If you don't want to wait around for the heir hunters to come to you, you can be your own detective.

You can contact your attorney general (to find your state attorney general, http://www.naag.org/) and there are several online sources for finding unclaimed inheritances, but be advised many of them want your money.

> The best, easiest and most reliable way to search is to check the unclaimed asset database for the states you think there could be money.

You know me and those upfront fees. I avoid them. There are some free sites to use that are very good. A retired airline pilot who found his wife had inheritance money due her started NUPN.com. He did some exploring and researching of his own, and then started a database to help others find their missing loot.

Take a visit to National Unclaimed Property Network http://nupn.com/

index.htm to get started. This site provides links to state and federal databases. I wish you could click directly from this book to each state to their search forms, but since you can't, go to this site and click on state data and then click on your state. You are taken directly to the unclaimed assets site. Very handy.

Another site to use is missingmoney.com as well as unclaimed. org. Those are the most helpful and don't charge a fee. Remember, we included a listing of every state unclaimed asset office in Appendix 1 in the back of this book.

If you know for certain that there is inheritance money out there that you haven't collected, you can hire a lawyer to find it and make sure it finds its way to you.

The best way NOT to be in the missing money situation is to keep track of assets. Make a list of what is owned and what the value is. Keep a list of stocks, bonds, bank accounts, insurance policies, etc., and keep it in a safe location where someone else knows about it. If you have it in a safety deposit box, make sure the key and instructions to open the box are evident upon death.

If you suspect there is money out there, ask your relatives about the possibilities and where to search for more information. The best, easiest and most reliable way to search is to check the unclaimed asset database for the states you think there could be money. Maybe Grandma lived in Arkansas for years and then moved to Wisconsin and then to New York. Check them all.

Before we move on, another piece of advice to take from this book is to make sure your will is always up to date. Keep records of your assets and holdings, and let someone close to you know where to find your records in the event of your death.

Many people die without detailed or organized financial records, so their heirs have no idea. Many people also die with no will or an outdated will. You can do your own will with online resources, too. You don't have to pay a lawyer. That savings is Free Money, too.

People do not always share this important information with their loved ones and they should. Many family members don't know that a policy exists or they don't know how to track it down.

One in three life insurance policies are not claimed. We need to change that. And now we know how and where to look, just in case.

CHAPTER 12

Class Action Suits

Class action suits are easy FREE MONEY!

You must have received a notice in the mail at one point or another, and read that you were entitled to a settlement from a class action lawsuit. What did you do with it? Most people throw the letter away!

That's throwing away cash.

There are many ongoing open settlements, all the time. What is a class action lawsuit? In very simple terms, you are among a class of people entitled to a portion of money to be received because a company did you wrong in some way.

Maybe a telephone company mischarged for years. A class action lawsuit can be brought against the telephone company. That means not that one person is suing, but that the suit is filed on behalf of all people who were affected. Everyone who paid their bills during that time frame of the overcharges is entitled to a refund of these charges in the class action suit.

In fairly recent memory, there was a suit filed against Wal-Mart on behalf of its employees and it became the largest class action suit in history.

When you get the letter in the mail that says you are part of a class action suit, do not toss it in the trash. There usually is a short form to fill out and return. Do it. What have you got to lose?

The settlement portion that comes your way could be a few bucks, or it could surprise you.

In addition to the suits where you are notified, you can actively search class action suits that might pertain to you. Visit www.topclassactions.com to connect with settlements, lawsuits and attorneys. This FREE site is a database of the suits going on and all those entitled to receive funds.

> For class action suits, you have to file your claim to collect.

It is amazing how many apply to the everyday, average consumer. As we go to press, there are 38 open lawsuits in which you may be eligible to submit a claim. Did you purchase some of those "toning" shoes? Check it out! Maybe your bank slammed you with an overdraft fee. Check it out! Maybe you installed some new windows and they leak. Check it out!

No doubt you've been involved with companies that have or had a class action suit brought against them. I know of checks issued for forty cents (no kidding), forty bucks and four thousand dollars.

This topclassactions.com web site continually monitors the suits and posts the open settlements and the deadline for claiming your Free Money. Settlement amounts vary greatly, but it can pile up. If this Free Money is yours… then take it!

You can sign up at the site to receive info, or just check in regularly to verify what may or may not apply to you.

For class action suits, you have to file your claim to collect. It's very simple. Follow the instructions on the web, or in the mail if you received something via our US Post Office.

Not many people follow through with the class action, and they are missing out. There was a class action suit against Ross Stores not too long ago. Five thousand people filed claims. Nearly ONE MILLION people were eligible and did not file a claim! Only five thousand out of one million! If you were in that one million, don't you wish you would've received your check for nearly $250? I know I'd want my check!

You can peruse the site to see what applies to you. If you ever get the opportunity to be the lead plaintiff (or the key plaintiff or a named plaintiff), that means more money for you. The court sees it as you being one of the first to bring the suit and assumes you are busy with the lawyers. That means you get paid bigger bucks and you get paid first. These kinds of cases usually range from $1,000 to $10,000 for the primary people named.

Not a bad gig. You can collect on an unlimited number of suits. Maybe your utility company owes you something, your bank or the company that produces your makeup. The suit could be anything.

For example, let's say you used Brand X mascara and it made your eyelashes fall out. You were not the only one. The thousands of women who lost their eyelashes filed a class action suit.

You could be a key plaintiff and get the big bucks. Even if you don't get in as a lead plaintiff, you still can collect Free Money. Collecting from all the suits that apply to you can certainly add up.

The federal government has a web site as well that you can use to check on the status of class action suits and the settlement dates. See www.sec.gov/divisions/enforce/claims.htm for more information.

You can review the lengthy list of companies that have class action activity to see if it affects you in any way. If so… file your claim!

Get that Free Money!

CHAPTER 13

Debt Cures

Let me turn you on to a different kind of Free Money.

Getting rid of debt is the same as getting more money.

You often hear someone say, "I paid off my car! I have Free Money every month now!" Or "I am done paying my kids' tuition and it's like I got a big fat raise." Whatever the situation, everyone realizes that not having that debt to pay any more is like money in the pocket to use for other desires.

Paying off debt is only one way to get rid of debt. I wrote the book on it, literally. Many of you may have read my book *Debt Cures*. If so, you know I am passionate about reducing or eliminating debt.

Debt Cures They Don't Want You to Know About — (www.debt-cures.com) is jam packed with methods and techniques to help you get your debt down fast. To give you a taste of what that book is all about, I will share some of the methods, because it's like Free Money. Getting out of debt means more money back in your wallet for you to spend on whatever you like.

Free Assistance

Anytime you can get something without paying for it, that is Free Money in your pocket. I do not mean shoplifting, of course, but getting free services from the government is a great source of Free Money.

> The government spends millions every year in free debt counseling.

The government spends millions every year in free debt counseling. I cannot control how the government spends its millions, but I can tell you what is out there and how you can take advantage of that assistance.

Check out www.hud.gov. And, while I am mentioning HUD, there is a chance that you could be entitled to a refund, if you had an FHA-insured mortgage. If you think HUD owes you a refund, visit www.hud.gov/offices/hsg/comp/refunds/ to find out for free.

There are also nonprofit debt counseling services that are FREE, like GreenPath (www.greenpath.com). A little later, I'll delve a lot more into all the assistance programs that are out there.

Your Own Assistance

My motto: All you need to reduce or eliminate your debt is you.

Some simple tips from all the debt and credit and finance gurus are all rolled up into one and presented to you here. Getting rid of debt equals Free Money… but not getting into debt is even better. Am I right?

A good place to begin is tackling your credit cards. For any card you carry a balance on, call the customer service 800 number. You are your own debt counselor. YOU will ask for a lower interest rate. It's that simple.

Follow my age-old script:

> "Hello, my name is Kevin Trudeau and I have been an account holder with you for many years. I see that my interest rate is now up to 15% and that is simply too high. I need a much lower rate. What is the best you can do for me?"

Just like dealing with a used car dealer, let them throw out the first number.

> "Well, Mr. Trudeau, I can reduce that rate to 11%."

They may or may not deal with you. You may have to ask to speak to the supervisor or manager.

> "Hmmm. 11%. I can get a better deal with the credit card offer that came in the mail today. If you can't meet or beat their rate, I will close my account with you and transfer my balance."

> "Let's see, how does 0% for six months sound and then 5% after that?"

> "Sounds great, thank you."

It may not go word for word like that, but believe me, deals like that happen every day. This simple tactic works and it can save you hundreds, maybe even thousands of dollars. Reducing your interest rate reduces your payment and your overall balance due.

But you have to pick up the phone and ask. That is tough for some folks, but think about it. Do you want to keep giving them Free Money or get Free Money for yourself?

Beat the Fees

The same rationale goes for fees. I hate fees. If we all had a dollar for every time I said that, this economy would be a different ballgame. You can reduce fees and keep some of that Free Money for yourself.

Again, pick up your secret weapon. The phone. YOU are now wearing the hat of your debt counselor. YOU are working for you, to get you more money.

Whatever the fee, you should call. If you got hit with a late fee or an over-the-limit fee or any kind of crazy fee that they throw at you, call them up. Call the bank or the credit card company and ask them to remove the fee.

Just like in the example above, be polite but be firm and consistent. And, "demand," ever so politely, that the fees be taken off your account. Ask to speak to a person higher up in the supervisory chain if need be. Explain why you were late this one time and how it was not a normal pattern, etc., etc., etc. Be a real person with a real story and you will probably get quicker results.

I often tell a story of one guy I know. He says he has a magic word. He was talking to the customer service representative at his credit card company, asking for the fee to be wiped off his account. Most of the time polite asking works, but this time, the customer service rep paused and asked: "Sir, are you demanding that the fees be removed?"

His intuition kicked in, and he replied, "Yes, I am. I demand it."

And guess what? This is what he was told: "Well, all right then, I will remove the fees from your account."

He is under the impression that, from his experience, the "rule book" at this particular company instructed customer service representatives to say no if the customer merely asked for fees to be waived, but if the customer demanded, then they removed the fee. The bottom line is don't lose the customer.

Different companies have different playbooks. Some are immediately helpful; some may make you work for it a little bit. Be persistent. What have you got to lose?

Stay in Control

The key is not to be intimidated. The customer service reps are people like you and me. They do not want to charge the fees… it's the banks and the credit card companies. Times are tough for them, too, so they are trying to beef up their revenues by sticking it to you any way they can.

> You can haggle on fees and interest rates, and you can negotiate to reduce the balance that you owe.

Credit card interest rates are being jacked up with no reason or warning. Credit limits are being reduced, again with no notice or justification, so they can hit you up with an over-the-limit fee. Any way they can devise to find a way to stick it to you with a fee, they will do it. It's a no mercy kind of gimmick.

But you don't have to sit back and take it. Remember, YOU are wearing the hat of the debt assistance counselor. YOU are the one to calmly take control of the situation. YOU routinely follow the game plan.

Rule number one is to review your statements every month.

Rule number two is to call right away to get rid of fees and high interest rates like we just discussed.

Rule number three is to negotiate the actual principle balance.

> Yes, you may be able to negotiate the amount you owe.

Yes, you may be able to negotiate the amount you owe. As I have said, these are drastic economic times. The reality is that this is the perfect time for negotiation.

You can haggle on fees and interest rates, and you can negotiate to reduce the balance that you owe.

I often use the example of Sally. Sally lost her job and was working part-time at a diner. She owed $3,000 on her credit card. The minimum monthly payment was too steep and the balance was only that high because every month, the interest piled up because she couldn't pay it off.

We all know that vicious cycle.

Sally made the call to reduce her interest rate and then it occurred to her to go a step further.

> Sally: "I have been laid off from my job for months now and my credit card balance keeps going up even though I am no longer charging on it. Because I paid less than the minimum payment, the fees and interest were more than the amount I paid. The bill is higher the next month even after I make a payment. It is nuts."

Sally had to get off the merry-go-round that was becoming more like an avalanche. She called her credit card company and got the minimum payment reduced and the fees waived and the interest rate lowered. That was quite a success and quite a money saver.

Riding on that success, Sally called the credit card company again.

"I have a balance of $3,000 and with my loss of work, I simply cannot pay it. The funds just aren't there. What I propose is that you remove from that balance all the accumulated past interest and fees. If we can get down to just the original purchases I made, I will be able to manage to pay it off."

The reply? "Okay."

For Sally, and for you, keeping your money is just like earning Free Money.

Seriously Folks

I've been telling that story so long and it never loses its impact. Sally was right to ask. Maybe your conversation won't happen quite that fast or quite that directly, but Sally was able to negotiate down to where she could pay… and so can you.

She was smart to explain her situation, what she could pay, and how the balance included so much more than the original bill. Never underestimate the power of a phone call. All that money that she ended up not paying is like Free Money, plain and simple.

This kind of negotiation can be applied to car loans, personal loans, etc. If you have balances on loans or credit cards, it's time to pick up the phone.

Bill Collectors

Where there is smoke, there is often fire, and where there is debt, there is often a bill collector. Collection agents are usually pretty yucky creatures and the economic climate has made them more devious, creating even more unscrupulous scoundrels.

If you have debt, there is one piece of advice that can make a big difference in your life: Do Not Fear the Debt Collector.

Folks who owe money are usually stressed out and their resistance is weak. Bill collectors like to take advantage of that fear. Let me clue you in to their ways so you know what tactics to use to ward them off.

I wrote this in the first *Free Money* book and it still holds true today. Who are the scoundrels? The bill collectors! Not the usual collection agency guys; they're bad enough. There is another breed on the loose that will do practically anything to get a buck out of you.

What these guys (and gals) do is buy up old accounts from credit card companies or collection agencies and they go after that old debt. They want you to think that they have the right to collect and that you have to pay them. Don't fall for it!

When it comes to debt collectors, any debt collectors, I offer two tips. Never give them any information. Don't even acknowledge the debt as yours.

There is so much mix-up and mess in the financial world; you could very well get a collection call on a debt that is not yours. NOT YOURS. So don't own up to it. There is so much pressure on debt collectors; they will resort to nefarious ways to get a buck. Do not fall for it. Do not get bullied by them.

"Alleged Debt"

If you are contacted by a collection agency, always refer to the debt as the "alleged debt." Don't say, "Oh yeah, that old account? Yes I know about it." No way.

Use sentences like:

"I have no knowledge of that alleged debt."

"That alleged debt does not appear to be in my records."

"You will have to provide me documentation of that alleged debt."

Never admit that it is yours. It may not be. Make them give you information in writing. Sometimes that is enough for them to back off. These goons want to deal with the people who are afraid of them because they think they can get more money that way.

Even if the debt was yours, it may now be old debt that is now too old for them to collect. Did you realize there is a time limit to collect old debts? There is. So again, that is another reason to always use the term "alleged debt."

Old Debt

Debt collectors are notorious for calling up people for old debt. This is how it sometimes works: The collectors buy old debt accounts for pennies on the dollar. The holder of the debt, the credit card company, long ago wrote off the account. They are not looking for you. The collectors are going to keep whatever they get from you. They have little invested, so it's a profit program for them.

Here's the important point to remember: the debt is uncollectible. They are going after money that you have no legal obligation to pay! They are banking on the fact that you won't know that. They are hoping you will be intimidated and turn over your dough.

Let's run through a tried and true example. You get a phone call from Callous Collector, who tries to put the squeeze on you for some debt that goes back a few years.

You have read this book and say you know nothing about the alleged debt.

If Callous Collector keeps at it, make him provide the detailed information on said account. If that's not enough, you may want to hit him with theses powerful words…"statute of limitations."

Statute of Limitations

Debt has a statute of limitations. That means there is a limit to how long they can come after you. In many states it is three years.

Many collectors try to get payment on accounts that have expired, and unknowing people panic when they call. Now you know you can't be backed into a corner. Don't be afraid. Be wise. Fight their scare tactics with the facts.

If you get another call from Callous Collector, say this: "The statute of limitations on this alleged debt is expired. Goodbye."

The collector will no doubt be surprised you know about statutes. But now you do and it's a beautiful thing. It doesn't matter the dollar amount. If the statute of limitations has expired, no one is able to force collection. Now, that's what I call a Free Money gift!

The statute period varies from state to state. We have included a chart in the Appendix section of this book of all the states and the statute of limitation periods. In many states, all it takes is just three years to be free from collection efforts. You can read more about this topic online or in the *Debt Cures* book.

CHAPTER 14

Free Money While You're Waiting on Money

As I've stated in my *Debt Cures* books and *Free Money* book, there are hundreds of ways to get more money into your life.

Using the Internet and the telephone are two quick and easy ways. My experience has always been… ask and you shall receive! Another great piece of advice… just do it!

Reducing your interest rate on a $9,000 credit card balance (the average American carries that much of a balance) from 20% to 10% can save you a thousand bucks. Calling your cable company and getting the best deal can save you hundreds. When it comes to car insurance, re-evaluate who drives and how far and how often. Can someone take public transportation? That can save you big bucks in lower insurance premiums, which will more than pay for the bus pass. And, you won't have to fill up the car quite so much.

House insurance? One call to tell your agent that you have updated your smoke detectors or done something energy efficient could mean a couple hundred bucks back to you. Do you have a cell phone? Does anybody else in your house? Get on a shared plan. And watch the minutes and the texting charges. If you know you're text crazy, get the unlimited. If not, check your usage during the past few months and check into a plan that makes sense for you. You can easily save hundreds per year by going with the shared plan… and by not paying for services you're not using.

There is free help in so many unexpected places. Free childcare? Yes, there is Grandma and your sister. Not paying daycare saves you hundreds. Don't have relatives nearby? Swap childcare with a neighbor.

Some Child and Family Service agencies have wheels-to-work programs. You may be able to find one in your community. Many of these programs are there to help fix an existing car or to finance a loan on a newer, more reliable vehicle. Catholic Charities also have wheels programs. See www.catholiccharities.org. Also check out www.goodwill.org. Certain states have their own programs. For example, New Hampshire has a comprehensive program. It includes transportation and reimbursement for expenses.

There are so many sources and resources. Keep your eyes and ears open all the time and you will be amazed at what's available.

Food 'n Stuff

Write down every dollar you spend. When you see where it's going, you'll become aware of many things you've been blowing your bucks on. When you stop these phantom expenses, you'll be amazed just how fast the savings add up each week.

Use restaurant.com to find deals. Use coupons. Just the tip of the iceberg here:

✔ fatwallet.com

✔ couponchief.com

✔ coolsavings.com

✔ Pricegrabber.com

✔ smartaboutmoney.org

Restaurants and stores all have birthday clubs and email clubs. Join! You get free stuff and free food and discounts. "Kids eat free on Tuesdays." If you go out to eat as a family, go on Tuesdays. "Senior discount before 5 p.m." Eat before 5 p.m. "Buy one entrée, get one free." Take advantage of advertised specials and unadvertised coupon deals.

If your situation is more serious and you need serious help, The United States Supplemental Nutritional Assistance Program (SNAP), also known as the Food Stamp Program, is a Federal Government Program providing assistance to zero and low-income people and families in the United States.

The U.S. Department of Agriculture oversees and administers the Food Stamp Program, but the individual states distribute the Food Stamp Benefits. GovBenefitsOnline.org can assist you in applying for your state Food Stamp Benefits and provide you information about additional benefits available to Food Stamp applicants.

Each state distributes food stamps. Department of Human Services is there for you to apply for other benefits, too. For example, the state of Illinois lists Medical Benefits, SNAP Benefits, Cash Assistance, Employment and Training Services, Alcohol and Substance Abuse Services, Domestic Violence Services, Mental Health Services, Services for Pregnant Women, Child Care Services, Women, Infants and Children (WIC), Services for Teen Parents, Child Support, Services for People with Disabilities, Group Care Nursing Homes, Services for Senior Citizens, LIHEAP, Earned

Income Tax Credit (EITC), Crisis Nursery, Food Pantries, Healthy Families Illinois and Homeless Services.

We'll feature government assistance elsewhere, but it's good to know how much is actually offered. Back to our food and stuff topic. For your favorite "stuff," go online to your favorite product web sites. Many send free coupons and/or free samples of hair care products, cleaning supplies, etc.

> For bigger "stuff," shop the returns, damaged and dented, and old models.

For bigger "stuff," shop returns, damaged, dented, or for old models. Last year's stove model is the same great stove for a lot less money. And if you're in the market for carpeting, check out the remnant section and you could save hundreds.

Do you have a small business? Need business cards or postcards or magnets? You can get these items for FREE at www. vistaprint.com. All you pay is the shipping.

How long has it been since you've utilized the library in your community? Take advantage of the Free Money available at your local library. Free books. Free newspapers. Free Internet. Free movies. Free music. Well, maybe they charge a quarter to check them out now.

Utility Help

Do you want FREE light bulbs? Many communities give free light bulbs. Charlotte, NC Duke Energy gave more than ten million compact fluorescent light bulbs in 2010 and continued the program in 2011. Swapping bulbs to CFLs uses 75% less energy and last up to ten times longer. Light bulbs aren't cheap, so getting them free is a great Free Money source and they save you money during the course of the year. Double bonus.

There is also free help for those who need assistance with their utility bills. Go to www.hud.gov. Some communities have assistance programs, too. There's an organization known as the Arizona Public Service (APS), and they have a program that helps low-income residents pay their energy bills. You can get a discount of up to 40% off, if you qualify. Take a look at the APS site, which can be found at: www.aps.com. You can also call 1-800-253-9405 to find out more about eligibility requirements. Call your local utility company to learn about programs specific to your area.

The Low Income Home Energy Assistance Program (LIHEAP) is a great place to go if you're looking for some funds to pay your energy bills. Run by the Division of Energy Assistance, the program is federally funded. Every year, money is distributed among all fifty states. Check to see what you can qualify for within your state. Get more information here: www.acf.hhs.gov/programs/ocs/programs/liheap.

You may be able to get help to pay your bills through Supplemental Security Income. SSI is not Social Security. Elderly, disabled, blind and low-income folks get money to pay their bills. Cash to meet basic needs... food, shelter and clothing... more than $600 for a single and $900 for a couple. The amounts are adjusted each year. See www.ssa.gov/ssi. It's a very helpful, easy to use web site.

There are even some states out there that will take it a step further and actually add to the benefits that SSI already gives you. So what you initially receive may increase even more. Not only that, if you qualify for SSI, you may also qualify for other services within your state.

House 'n Stuff

The Rural Housing Repair Loans and Grants can give you the Free Money or the low cost loan you need to help you with improving your home. Through their program, you can potentially receive more than $7,000 in Free Money. This is a US Department of Agriculture program and you can get all the details, including more information about the application process at: www.benefits.gov and www.rurdev.usda.gov/LP_Subject_HousingAndCommunityAssistance.html.

Do you know you can get money for your car repairs? For example, a New Hampshire program gives out $500 if you meet their requirements. See www.dhhs.nh.gov for Free Money to fix your car. This is just one example of what's out there in various states.

There are programs to send your kids to preschool for free. Head Start has been around for years. Go to www.nhsa.org to get more information.

You may be able to get government money to pay for your parking. Up to $230 per month. See irs.gov/pub/irs-pdf/p15b.pdf. (IRS Pub 15-B (2009) Page 20.) There is even a benefit if you commute by bicycle. Subject to rules, you can get $20 per month.

What if you're looking for a job and you need an outfit to wear to the interview, but don't have the money to buy new clothes? Most every state or community has a program to provide free clothes. Contact: www.dressforsuccess.org and www.bottomlessclosetnyc.org/ for a new FREE outfit for your interview.

Victims of crime can get up to $10,000, even $25,000 in compensation through various state programs. The Federal Office makes the grants to states for Victims of Crime (OVC). Theft, damage and property loss are not usually covered. See www.ojp.usdoj.gov/ovc for more information.

Most funds come from two pools of money: victim compensation and victim assistance. For example, in Colorado, contact www.coloradocrimevictims.org.

Do you see what I mean? Money for nearly every topic you can think of. We will get to the topic of grants, too. Grants are a prime source of Free Money.

Many grant applications can be done online. Follow the instructions, step by step. Different grants ask for different things. If you have questions, you can contact that agency directly. Most have help sections on their web sites to guide you through the process.

For the federal government agency directory, contact: www.usa.gov for contact information. There is also a giant book, if you want paper to read. It's 2,400 pages. Detailed grant information is printed in the Catalog of Federal Domestic Assistance and is available for $75. You can order it from the US Government Bookstore at http://bookstore.gpo.gov/ ... or you can just keep reading this book.

Good Go-To Info

To find your state housing authority office:

✔ www.ncsha.org/

To find your state attorney general:

✔ http://www.naag.org/

To find who is representing you in Congress:

✔ www.congress.org

Turn Your Trash into Treasure

Sometimes Free Money is literally lying around your house. Something that really gets people fired up is the ability to make big bucks really quickly. The skeptics start out with doubt written all over their face, but they soon become huge proponents because these methods work.

I heard from a gal who read about this method in the first *Free Money* book. She is going crazy (good crazy) making money. She could not be happier.

> Turn your trash into treasure.

This particular woman decided to clean out the garage. She sold a bunch of stuff. She made a mint. That got her so excited that she cleaned out the basement and the attic. More huge dollars! She couldn't stop. She cleaned out her closets.

Getting rid of all the stuff she didn't use made her feel lighter in every way. Less clutter is a happier way to live. Any self-help expert will tell you that. But the thrill of making fistfuls of money was her real happiness. It was so easy and she made thousands.

Another reader is a compulsive shopper. She can't stop herself from going to sidewalk sales, outlet malls, clearance sales, flea markets, yard sales, auctions, estate sales and antique stores. She is a treasure hunter. But she's also a treasure seller!

The thrill of the hunt and the find was her hobby. She loves it. But she was getting buried in stuff. She learned she could turn a hefty profit very quickly and that's her new past time. She loves making money with very little investment and it's fun for her.

I have heard of men who do the same with baseball cards, tools and old junk. Finders aren't just keepers… finders are sometimes sellers who make big bucks. That old beer can collection could be a veritable gold mine.

There's another gal who told us about how she made $12,000 in one day! Tammy Allen has been collecting pottery all her life. She loves the hobby and buys it cheaply every chance she gets. One day, the guy who mows her grass noticed some of the pottery in her living room and told her that he knows a man who collects the same stuff and would buy her collection.

Tammy wasn't ready to sell, but a year later, she gave him a call. He paid her $12,000 in cash! Tammy was like a lot of people, living paycheck to paycheck. That huge payday was a thrill. She and her husband had been losing sleep worrying about how they were going to pay for their daughter's tuition at dental school and now they had their answer.

Tammy's husband had claimed her collection was worthless, but it was really worth thousands. Another benefit surprised Tammy. She now had more room in her home for entertaining and it felt really good to welcome friends and family back into their home. She claimed the treasure sale was like a double-edged sword that was beautiful on both sides.

She has since learned to apply her trash to treasure technique whenever she wants money. Tammy has taught her mom the same method. Her mom made $20,000 in one day by selling items and collectibles she had at her house. That was a major income boon to a retired lady on a fixed income.

Tammy loves to spend her weekends treasure hunting and even finds things that others discard that are worth money. Finding that diamond in the rough is a thrill. Tammy says she spends next to nothing. She now knows that she can make fast, easy money with this one fast, easy method. She loves to share this method and tells people that you don't have to have a lot of money to make a lot of money. Tammy also advises people to look for things that they already have at home that could be worth money.

> She has since learned to apply her trash to treasure technique whenever she wants money.

The sale of her pottery collection got her started and now she sells other collectibles and items, turning them into cold hard cash. Collecting is her passion and her joy. Now that Tammy makes money from it, it brings her even more joy. As she puts it, she took something she loved and turned it into a windfall for her family.

Doing What You Love

There are so many ways to make quick, easy cash. There are many readers out there who can tell you that these tips work. This list will ignite your creativity and get you thinking of ways to make money that you previously didn't imagine.

I know of people who walk dogs, bathe dogs and even pick up dog poop. They love it (even the dog poop guy) and they get fast cash. Doing a little activity that you enjoy and making money at it… there's magic in that.

In fact, I know a guy who does magic tricks at a local restaurant and makes a pretty penny. I know a gal who ties balloon animals at the pancake house and makes a pretty penny. I know a lot of people who do a lot of fun stuff and make a pretty penny.

eBay

Playing on eBay is another fun way to earn money. I don't get any kickbacks or love money or anything for talking about eBay. It's simply hands-down an easy and sure-fire way to put some fast greenback in your wallet.

I could write a book on how to use eBay, but I imagine there are already books out there that serve that purpose. Take a look around your house. Go through the garage. Spend an hour in the attic. What's been sitting in your basement for years that you forgot you even had? If you're a "normal" American, you hang on to stuff for the eternal reason... "just in case I need it someday." We end up with a lot of stuff that we never use. I know a guy who keeps everything, but when he needs it, he can't find it. So he goes out and buys another one. He has two sets of painting supplies, two sets of tools... you get the idea.

Even if you are not a stockpiler, a hoarder or an unorganized "where did I put that?" kind of person, I can guarantee that you have stuff you can get rid of. We all do. Think of that stuff as cash in your pocket and it'll make it easier to let it go.

> If you can see that your stuff really is cash in your pocket, it makes it easier to part with.

Got golf clubs that you haven't used in three years? Get rid of them. Maybe it's a bike or roller blades? If you have kids, you have a never-ending turnover of stuff that you can get rid of when they outgrow it or tire of it. Famous brand children's clothing makes a killing on eBay. Their toys, your toys, your tools, the possibilities are endless.

The beauty of eBay is how easy it is and how easy it is for you to get paid. Set up a PayPal account (it's quick and easy and requires no technical savvy), and the payments you receive are deposited right into your PayPal account. You don't have to deal with credit cards or worry if the buyer's check is going to bounce. You just sit back and watch the balance in your account go up, up, up.

Craigslist

Another great Internet gold mine is craigslist. There really is a guy named Craig who started an online version of a buy it/sell it bulletin board. Remember in college when people would post little notes by the campus mailbox? "Need a ride to San Diego this weekend." "Have a motorcycle to sell." "Looking for a roommate this summer?"

The concept is the same, but the venue has gone global. If you have something to offer, I guarantee there is someone looking for it and they look on craigslist. Go to www.craigslist.com and check it out. The possibilities for Free Money are endless.

Sell your car, motorcycle, scooter, boat, Winnebago RV, your electronics, your jewelry or your collectibles. If you have a vacation home, rent it for a week and make big bucks fast.

If you live in New York or any other cool place that people want to visit, rent out your apartment for a week and get quick cash. It's amazing the transactions that can happen when you use your creative mind.

Facebook and twitter

Social media is a great way to advertise what you want to sell. Be it old baby clothes or fishing tackle, someone wants your stuff. Maybe you are breeding puppies now. You can have them sold before they're even born. Maybe you want to offer your services as a singing telegram person. Post it on Facebook and you could be raking in the cash sooner than you think. This free word of mouth media has revolutionized the Free Money world.

YouTube

Whatever it is you do… whatever it is you want… whatever it is you want to say, share, get or receive… make a quick video and post it for free on YouTube. You can make a video with your camera, your phone or a Flip Video. Uploading is easy. If you have a web site, post your video there. You can make a simple web site for free, or practically free, as well. You can post your video on Facebook and twitter. I bet you could make money asking for people to send you money and people would do it.

Sell your car

You can use eBay or craigslist or any other online site. You can set it in front of your house with a For Sale sign. You can run an ad in your local paper. You can take it to a used car lot and see what they will give you. You can simply tell a friend to tell everyone he knows that you have a car for sale.

Word of mouth is often the best way to get things done and costs you nothing. If you live in a metropolitan area with good public transportation, you honestly do not need a car. I know of a gal who lives in Chicago about a block from the train station. She walks to everything in her local neighborhood and when she needs a car, there's a car rental place just a few blocks away. She can walk there and rent a car for just as long as she needs, even just for an afternoon.

The money she spends to rent a car on occasion is much less than the cost of car payments, insurance and maintenance. And she doesn't hassle with parking. If you ever lived in a big city, you know how irritating that can be.

Maybe you simply can't live without your car. Or you think you can't anyway. I suggest letting the idea gel for a while. Motor scooters are a great transportation alternative. And when you need to take a long road trip, borrow a buddy's wheels. Or call the rental guys. If you only need wheels for an occasional road trip, renting makes sense.

If you have a boat, you can sell it and get a large chunk of change immediately. Are you an avid boater? If not, think about how much you spend on the watercraft and how much enjoyment you get out of it. If you're in a climate where you only have three months of boating weather, and you're paying for storage the other nine months, selling your boat makes double sense.

Sell your collections

Most folks have something that they have been hanging on to for years. Then, they reach a point in their lives when their interests change, and those collections no longer mean as much to them. Are you a collector? Then there is cash to be had.

The baseball cards you've been collecting since you were a kid have value. If the sentimental value is no longer there for you, it's time to cash in. There are other collectors out there that want your stash.

I know of a guy who is a collector of old and rare coins. He makes great money selling to stores and other collectors. There are all kinds of collectibles out there: stamps, postcards, antique toys, trinkets and glassware from different eras. If your passion is Depression glass or Victorian silver, there's a market.

> People make great money at flea markets and antique shows and estate sales.

People make great money at flea markets and antique shows and estate sales. However, you must realize that you are investing some upfront money. Unless you have a guaranteed buyer, the first sale may take some time, so there is a risk factor.

Also, remember the market is fickle. People are into one thing and then something else becomes hot. I know of folks who made a fortune on Beanie Babies years ago, but that trend eventually died. Sell during the right time, and you make Free Money. Sell at the wrong time, and you have a basement full of furry critters.

Take a loan against your 401(k)

If you have a nice nest egg in the retirement account, but you need money right here, right now, think about taking a loan against your 401(k). You get the money fast, and you get a good interest rate. Best of all, you're paying yourself back, not a bank.

Take a loan against other investment accounts

The same logic applies here as well. Quick, liquid cash available when you need it. Pay yourself back at a good rate.

Phone a friend

Do you have a friend or relative who owes you money? Now is the time to collect. Or maybe you have a friend or relative who once offered you a loan. If you want quick cash in a jiffy, accept the loan with heartfelt thanks. Maybe they will even give it to you interest free.

Get an advance from your employer

Depending upon your type of work and method of payment, you may be able to get an advance from your employer. If you know you have a good commission check coming next month, think about taking it as an advance now, if you need the funds pronto.

Equity line

If you're a homeowner, access your home equity line of credit. You can get big sums, pay little interest and you get the cash you need. Equity lines usually have the cheapest interest rate (so not entirely Free Money, but fast money). You may even be able to deduct the interest on the loan… and that IS Free Money.

Consult

Use your expertise to make a quick buck. Find consulting jobs that pay an advance. You need fast cash, and people need what you know. Find a consulting job by word of

mouth or online at www.csc.com, www.careerbuilder.
com or at http://operations-jobs.theladders.com/.

Licensing

License your product or idea to an infomercial company.
Infomercial companies are often willing to see you on
short notice and move aggressively (if they like your
product). Many are willing to pay $10-30,000 just for
licensing, plus a royalty.

Audition

Audition for modeling opportunities. No, not "those
kind" of gigs. There are legitimate needs for print and
video ads. Television commercials need local people.
Maybe you can audition for acting parts as well.

Your House

Do you live in a town where things happen? Super Bowl,
Final Four or Olympics? Rent out your house during
that week. People will pay huge money! There are online
sites to market your house for you.

Go for the Gold

When I talk about there being a gold mine of opportunities out there for you to get quick cash, I mean it. People
are having gold parties these days at their homes. Turn
in your old outdated gold jewelry and get big money
that night. Visit www.cash4gold.com and turn that old
gold into Free Money.

Finder's Fees/Assignment of Contract

Creativity is key here; so let your imagination be your guide and you can make sums like you never imagined. Finder's fees, referral fees and assignment of contract can be a veritable cash gold mine.

An assignment of contract occurs when a party to a contract hands off his rights to it to another party. An easy legal explanation goes like this: Joe contracts with Water Company Works to bring a jug of water to his office every day. Water Company Works assigns the contract to Wonderful Water World. Joe still gets his water every day, he is happy.

> Finder's fees/ referral fees/ assignment of contract, ah, a veritable cash gold mine.

That's swell, but how does this work for you to make money. Say Lucy contracted with Jack to mow her grass for $25. Jack then assigns the contract to Mike. Lucy pays $25 and her lawn gets mowed. Jack takes a fee and Mike gets paid to mow the grass. Jack is like a middleman. He does not want to mow grass, but he is good at finding people who need their lawns mowed. Mike likes to mow, but does not like to deal with people. Win-win-win.

Assignment of contract can be as simple or as complicated as you make it. I like to keep things simple. For more info and resources, check out www.nolo.com and www.4lawschool.com.

Finder's fees are similar in concept, but no contract is involved. You get a fee for being the guy who matches up the seller and the buyer. Say that you know a guy with a garage full of whirly gigs. You find a girl who wants to buy whirly gigs. You bring the two of them together. They both get what they want and the gratitude to you comes in the means of cold hard cash.

It's a beautiful thing. You are finding a buyer for someone else. They appreciate that. They pay you. Life is good.

Hopefully, these ideas get your creative juices flowing and you are now open to all the possibilities to earn Free Money while you're waiting on other Free Money!

CHAPTER 15

Foreclosures

The foreclosure crisis is the longest running crisis I've ever heard of. Usually a crisis is a temporary, passing event. This fiasco has been dragging on for years.

The silver lining in this dark economic cloud is the Free Money that can come of foreclosures. In fact, there is so much opportunity in this area I should write an entire book on the subject.

For this book, we'll give highlights to make you aware of the vast potential of the foreclosure market.

A Glut on the Market

The banks went foreclosure crazy and foreclosures have hit record highs. We can rant and rave about how the whole mess started and I often do. The point is that there are many homes on the market now and prices in most markets are still dirt-cheap. The banks can't keep up with the inventory, and amazing deals are available in nearly every community across the country.

This is what I wrote in the first *Free Money* book: "Since this whole mortgage crisis hit, a record number of foreclosures take place every month. Nearly 1.4 million homes have been foreclosed on since July 2007."

Some experts say we may be experiencing the beginning of a recovery, but when you look at the total numbers, the foreclosure crisis still looks like a crisis to me. The bigger picture numbers show a lot of foreclosure activity. I just pulled this information:

RealtyTrac, the leading online marketplace for foreclosure properties, released its Year-End 2011 U.S. Foreclosure Market Report. It showed a total of 2,698,967 foreclosure filings (default notices, scheduled auctions and bank repossessions) were reported on 1,887,777 U.S. properties in 2011, a decrease of 34 percent in total properties from 2010.

Foreclosure activity in 2011 was 33 percent below the 2009 total and 19 percent below the 2008 total.

The report also showed that 1.45 percent of U.S. housing units (one in 69) had at least one foreclosure filing during the year, down from 2.23 percent in 2010, 2.21 percent in 2009, and 1.84 percent in 2008.

Since the first *Free Money* book was written, MILLIONS of homes have been foreclosed. Every state has been hit hard. The hardest hit in the nation are Nevada, Arizona, Florida and California.

The point to remember in all of this is that the banks have too many houses on their books. They don't want to be in the real estate business. They want to unload these properties. And that means prices are at record lows.

Houses on the Cheap

If you are in the position to buy, this is a buyers' market. Never before have there been prices like this. The home prices now are like from decades ago.

There are many ways to approach the foreclosure "issue" and we are looking at it from a Free Money aspect. Buying a house for practically nothing is a great Free Money investment. There are still ways to get a house with no money down and there are ways to get a house with almost no money.

Ever heard of a house for sale for a grand? It is real. Try buying a car for $1,000 and you will be surprised, but who ever thought you could buy a house for $1,000 in this day and age? I kid you not.

A reporter from CNN did a little research to show how amazingly low the prices are and houses were found for pennies. In January of 2009, CNNMoney.com did a report on bargain foreclosure properties. By simply pulling up the popular web site, www.realtor.com, the reporter searched for homes that had a list-selling price for less than $3,000.

> Realtor.com has a button on the search page dedicated to foreclosures.

Realtor.com has a button on the search page dedicated to foreclosures:

> Flint, Michigan: 12 houses; one as low as $6,000. Florida City, Florida: 12 properties listed; one as low as $36,900. Los Angeles, California: 68 properties.

To check on properties near you, type in your city and see what foreclosure deals exist. A quick click of Chicago, IL and limiting the price to under $5,000 revealed 21 homes. That's crazy. Even in the 1980s or 1990s, did you ever think you could buy a home anywhere for $5,000?

Or could you ever think you could nab a house in Sacramento, California for under $30,000? At the time of printing this book, there are 41. California is the land of million dollar homes. California is also now the home of foreclosure bargains.

Using the web site realtor.com, or zillow.com or trulia.com… any other site that you like… you can find homes in your area, too.

The Flip

Most of these homes will need a little maintenance and maybe some fixing up to get ready for resale, or to live in, but even factoring in those repair costs, there is money to be made in the foreclosure market.

The banks just want to unload these homes. There are simply too many and the banks are not making money by holding on to them. You, however, can make lots of money by making smart purchases.

If you can scoop up a house for less than $5,000 and put in another $20,000 in rehab expenses, you can turn around and sell it for twice or maybe three times that price.

There are still bargains to be had in every state.

The same CNN story reported a home for sale for under $2,000 that had suffered fire damage, but had a nice lot and was in a good area close to downtown. Other homes in that area sold for $100,000.

Think about the profit that could come from a small investment in fixing up such a property. Even if you spent $50,000 in renovations—which you probably wouldn't have to—you could still DOUBLE YOUR MONEY!

Perhaps the phrase often used, "the banks are giving properties away," is not so farfetched after all. Even in high priced areas, price tags drop by six digits in a jiffy.

Even when you have to pay a little more for a bargain home, you literally can make a fortune in foreclosures.

You don't need education to get started. You can negotiate anything. You can buy a property with virtually no money out of your pocket. You can sell it or keep it for rental income. The amount of investment is up to you. There is always risk involved when you play the real estate game. If you have a buyer lined up, great! If not, you may have to wait it out a bit. But all that Free Money at the end may be well worth the wait.

Think about Lisette and all the others who had no real experience in the real estate market. They took advantage of the current situation of the market full of foreclosed homes and turned it into a profit making payday for themselves.

I know it is possible for you, too.

Government Assistance

Jump online and start perusing the web sites. Home prices in many cities are still ridiculously low. Right now, you can get a home in the historic district of Savannah, Georgia for less than $85,000. If you ever considered living in a quaint, historic district, now is the time.

It's not just the dirt-cheap prices that make buying now so lucrative. Not only can you purchase at unbelievably low prices, you may be able to get money from the government for the rehab repairs.

In some states, you can get money to spruce up your house and help blighted neighborhoods bounce back. In other states, they're doing the work and then turning over the homes.

The Neighborhood Stabilization Program (NSP) was created by Congress to give funding to all fifty states to distribute to counties and cities to help buy, fix up and sell all the abandoned and foreclosed properties that are taking over neighborhoods. HUD gives out the money to the NSP and the communities decide what redevelopment projects to take on. To apply for assistance, go to http://hudnsphelp.info/index.cfm and start exploring.

Currently, there are case study videos highlighting the great work being done across the country in places like Columbus, Ohio; Lake Worth, Florida; Pima County, Arizona; and Orange County, California.

> Millions of dollars have been poured into this program. Total funding $970 million.

You can play around on the web site to see what's going on in your state. They post reports every quarter. If your neighborhood is "troubled," you might see some of this grant money fixing up homes in your area. Maybe you can even get some for your home.

The US Department of Housing and Urban Development (HUD) also has loan programs for foreclosed properties. One of the programs offered through HUD is to finance the rehab and the home loan with one mortgage. This saves the homeowner time and money. The types of improvements that borrowers may make using Section 203(k) financing include:

✔ Structural alterations and reconstruction

✔ Modernization and improvements to the home's function

✔ Elimination of health and safety hazards

✔ Changes that improve appearance and eliminate obsolescence

- ✔ Reconditioning or replacing plumbing; installing a well and/or septic system

- ✔ Adding or replacing roofing, gutters, and downspouts

- ✔ Adding or replacing floors and/or floor treatments

- ✔ Major landscape work and site improvements

- ✔ Enhancing accessibility for a disabled person

- ✔ Making energy conservation improvements

You can download a brochure with all the details direct from the HUD web site. Another program via HUD is available to American Indian and Alaska Natives, making it possible for them to obtain financing for purchasing and/or rehabbing a home.

HUD guarantees the loans; so traditional lenders are more accommodating to these groups. As of 2010, this program has been involved with 12,000 loans and $2 billion in backing funds.

Another link from the HUD site leads to the USDA, which offers programs for rural land and homeowners. Rural Americans can also get help with their loans.

Offerings include rural housing guaranteed loans; rural housing direct loans; mutual self-help loans and rural housing site loans. Several grants are offered as well. Why do we love grants? Because they never, ever need to be repaid!

One such grant is the rural rehabilitation grant. Some grants have age and/or other requirements, but the funding is substantial.

Contact your local HUD office or visit www.hud.gov for details for your area/situation. Let your fingers do the walking. Clicking around online often leads to many new wonderful sources of Free Money.

CHAPTER 16

Your House

You may not have thought of it this way, but your house is a source of Free Money. There are several techniques that can allow your home to put money in your pocket.

Home Equity

Some people think that a home equity line is what I am talking about. I have nothing against home equity loans or home equity lines of credit. That can be a great way to get quick liquid cash.

If you go that route, just remember that the amount has to be paid back at some point, so make sure you get the best interest rate possible.

There are other ways that your house can be your haven and a nest of money, too. How about reducing your house payments? Every month you spend hundreds of dollars, maybe even thousands, on your mortgage. What if you paid less every month? That would be exciting!

Extra money to pay off other bills. Extra money to put toward your kids' education. Extra money to take a vacation. The list of possibilities goes on and on.

There are ways to reduce that house payment. One way is to refinance. Get a better rate and get a lower payment.

Loan Modification

You could also go for a loan modification.

What is that?

It's an adjustment to your loan to lower your payment. Sometimes a loan modification is temporary and sometimes it's not. Your lender might change terms for a few years, or for the remainder of the life of your loan. The idea is to get you into a mortgage payment that you can afford every month so you don't go into default and get tangled up in the foreclosure mess.

There are different ways to go about loan modification. Obviously, the first step is to talk to your lender. Some loans will be given a new modified lower rate, for example from 8% down to 6%, for a limited time frame, perhaps the next five years. That reduction in interest rate makes a reduction in your payment.

> It's an adjustment to your loan to lower your payment.

Some loans may get spread out over a longer time period. Instead of a 30-year mortgage, some lenders are doing 40-year loan terms now. A 40-year loan at 5% is a nicely reduced lower payment and extra money in your bank account every month.

Lenders are more willing to work with you on modifying your existing mortgage these days because of all the foreclosures. They don't want any more foreclosures. Thousands of homeowners have received mortgage modifications or repayment plans from their lender.

In case you are wondering about the difference between refinance and modification: refinance is paying off the old loan by opening a brand new loan. It requires a new closing and paperwork, which means closing fees and title fees and all that other garbage banks charge for. A loan modification is simply making changes to your current existing loan to make it more manageable.

A CNNMoney.com story reported that "the mortgage lending industry is responding to the needs of its customers and offering solutions that are appropriate to the current market and economic conditions," said Hope Now's director Faith Schwartz.

Hope Now is the coalition of lenders, investors and community advocacy groups who have joined together "to combat the foreclosure plague." (Source: money.cnn.com/2009/03/30/real_estate/February_Hope_Now/index.htm?postversion=2009033013)

It's been a while since the first *Free Money* book first appeared and these words still are true: If ever the market was ripe for mortgage loan modification, for better or worse, now is that time. The economy is still struggling. People still fear for their jobs. Take note: you need to have employment in order to get the loan modified in most cases.

Follow the thought process. A person can't make his house payment. He modifies the loan in order to get a lower payment. He then makes his payment and doesn't go into default. The foreclosure process will not be necessary and the banks can still collect their dough, and the homeowner can stay in his house. Both parties are satisfied.

Because of the crash of the economy and the onslaught of fore-closures, loan modifications are becoming very popular. The loans are actually getting modified, and it's not just an "Oh yeah, we'll give you a couple more months to catch up."

The government's housing plan gives money to the banks to subsidize the banks giving a lower interest rate to you. Too bad they didn't give that money directly to the homeowners.

Forbearance

There is also something else called a forbearance agreement. If you're having trouble making your payments, you may be able to get a forbearance agreement, which is a temporary suspension of your payments for a few months. Hopefully, in that few months, you will get back on track and be able to make regular monthly payments again.

As long as you have a job, the odds for modifying your loan are in your favor. The federal government passed a bill in March 2009 for hurting homeowners. The Making Home Affordable Program, according to the LA Times, "provides $75 billion in financial incentives to lenders so that they will reduce interest payments." Learn about what options might apply to you at www. makinghomeaffordable.gov.

In some cases the program allows for a reduction in principal so that the monthly payment will not exceed 31% of the borrower's income, but that reduction is only temporary. The set-aside portion of the principal will have to be repaid when the loan is paid off or refinanced or the house is sold. According to program guidelines: "It's for homeowners who have experienced a significant change in income or expenses to the point that the current mortgage payment is no longer affordable."

Free HUD Services

If you think you want to modify your loan, first talk to a mortgage counselor at your local HUD office. Their services are FREE. Find the local office at www.hud.gov. The counselor will review your income and your current mortgage and be able to determine if you are a candidate for a loan modification.

Then, make an appointment with your lender. New terms for your mortgage loan means extra money for you.

A word of caution must be given here. Because things are the way they are, a lot of people are scared of losing their homes. And when there is fear, there are predators out there willing to take advantage of that fear.

You do not need to pay anyone to renegotiate your mortgage loan for you. A whole new industry has popped up. These guys are charging big bucks to talk to your bank for you. You do not need anyone to talk for you! You sure as heck don't need to pay thousands of dollars for this "service."

Please note that there are legitimate nonprofit organizations out there that will help with your loan renegotiation, and they may charge a very small fee. To find a nonprofit agency in your area, contact your local HUD office or visit www.hud.gov. If someone plans to charge you three to five grand, they're not a nonprofit agency. They're definitely a profit agency, and they're trying to make that profit off of you.

There are no federal laws regulating this new field, so "buyers beware." Don't waste your precious money and your precious time with these so-called loan modification services. You can pick up the phone just as well as they can.

Many states are getting complaints about the service from people who turned over big bucks and nothing happened.

If you feel a little intimidated about the whole loan process, talk to your local HUD office. HUD has more than 2,300 nonprofit agencies nationwide that specialize in housing counseling.

"Magic Words"

While I'm on the subject of mortgages and fighting off foreclosures, there is a tactic you need to know about. It's been all over the news because it works. If you're in the midst of foreclosure proceedings, you can stave off the final blow with three little words: "Produce the note."

The banks are saying, "Pay up." You need to fire back with, "Show up." They need to show the legal document—your mortgage—and many times they can't do so. If they can't provide the paper, they have no proof.

This is not typically a permanent fix, but it gives you time. The courts are swamped with foreclosure cases. Most judges prefer the quick, clean cases. If your case has a snag, it may be pushed to the bottom of the pile.

> This is not typically a permanent fix, but it gives you time.

While the bank is searching for the proof of your mortgage, you're awarded time. That's precious time to come up with some money to pay the delinquent house payment or to renegotiate the terms of your mortgage. Most mortgages are not held by the bank that issued your original loan. The banks bundle up the loans into investment packages and sell them off. Your paperwork can easily go missing as it changes hands.

So when you are approached with a foreclosure notice, you simply say, "Show me the note." This tactic may buy you the time to save your house.

Housing Help

Maybe you are not facing foreclosure. Maybe you just want to dip into your home for some found money. With a traditional thirty-year mortgage, a homeowner ends up paying about double the purchase price of the home. That's a lot of money going to interest and into the bank's pocket, instead of yours. It's possible to pay off that 30-year mortgage in much less time! That means more money for you!

Obviously, you can pay more on the principal each month. Any extra towards the principal balance reduces the amount that the interest is calculated on. Some people pay double payments every month. Some folks throw an extra hundred in with their payment each month. Most of us, however, can only afford to make our current payment.

One trick is to take your existing mortgage payment and split it up into weekly payments. What could be easier than that! Paying bills by the week is often the best thing for people on a tight budget to do anyway.

Let's take the example of Jake. His mortgage payment of $4,000 is due the first of every month. Most mortgage loans allow for prepayment, so what Jake learned to do was split the $4,000 into weekly installments of $1,000 each. He is allowed to prepay, and he doesn't want to pay late and get charged a late fee. For his

> One trick is to take your existing mortgage payment and split it up into weekly payments.

payment due August 1, Jake makes weekly payments of $1,000 on July 7, July 14, and July 21, and then the final payment on August 1. He has made his entire payment by August 1, so there is no late fee.

It doesn't seem like it should make any difference at all, paying your mortgage this way, but it makes a tremendous difference. The amount of interest that you pay is greatly reduced each month because the bank or mortgage firm is getting a good portion of their payment early. You are not paying nearly as much interest, and more is going toward paying your principal.

You can shave years and years off the life of your mortgage! That is THOUSANDS OF DOLLARS in Free Money!

Another quick and easy method is to make just one extra mortgage payment each year toward your principal. If you don't think this will amount to much… think again! By making this extra payment, you could shave as much as three years off of a 20-year fixed rate mortgage. That's thousands of dollars in savings by simply making an extra payment toward your principal every year! This simple method will keep you years ahead of the game!

Pay off that mortgage sooner

- ✔ Get a loan from a family member to pay down the principal. The interest savings will allow you to repay.

- ✔ If you pay points on your loan, pay them up front. Don't roll them into the loan. If you're not paying them up front, you'll be stuck with a higher balance that you'll be paying interest on each month.

✔ Consider a loan from your 401(k) plan to pay down your mortgage. If you can get a lower rate than your mortgage, it's a good tactic. And you're paying yourself back.

Use your home as a forced savings account. Make a higher payment each month; for example, put $500 more directly toward the principal. You build up your equity faster and decrease the interest. If you need money, instead of having it sit in a savings account, you use a home equity loan or a home equity line of credit.

Mortgage Accelerator Loan

Ever heard of a mortgage accelerator loan? These loans use special accounts to encourage borrowers to apply all extra money toward their mortgages. The savings can be huge.

If you'd like to pay off that mortgage, but you lack the discipline to do so, a mortgage accelerator loan may be a great idea for you. All you have to do is refinance your home and set up an equity line of credit. The final step is to arrange it so that your paychecks from work are directly deposited into your new credit account. It's much like your regular checking account, with one distinct advantage: the money in the account reduces the balance of the mortgage and any money not paid for bills is applied against the principal balance.

With this special loan, your principal balance is decreased, and you end up saving bundles of interest! So, in essence, your paycheck goes toward paying off the house. There are currently two companies that offer this loan in the US. For more information, you can check it out at: http://www.debthelp.com/kc/317-mortgage-accelerator-loans.html.

Lower Your Rate

I always preach that getting that lower interest rate is the most amazing thing you can do to cut time and dollars off of your mortgage. Let's take a look at what happens with differing interest rates on a $200,000 mortgage.

Interest Rate	Payment	30 Years of Interest
9.3%	$1,651	$394,362
8.5	$1,542	$355,200
7.3	$1,373	$294,247
6.1	$1,220	$239,250
5.6	$1,151	$214,518
5.5	$1,136	$208,853

Is it obvious from looking at the chart? If you have 5.5% interest rate, your monthly payment is $1,136. Over thirty years, you would pay a total of $208,853 in interest.

If you have an interest rate of 8.5%, your monthly payment is now $1,542. That means every month, you pay more than $400 more, and that totals almost five grand in a year!

Here's what really hits home. Over the life of the loan, you would pay out $146,347 extra! Think of what all that money could be used for or invested in! That's almost $150,000. The mortgage loan amount of this example used to run the numbers is for a $200,000 mortgage. You could have bought another house!

PMI

Another way to put money back in your pocket is to get rid of PMI, private mortgage insurance. If you did not put 20% down on your house, the bank charged you PMI, just another way to squeeze money out of you.

Apply all the ways you know (and from this book) to make quick cash and put money toward your equity to get you up to 20%. PMI is literally throwing money away each month.

You can also get your home reappraised to see if the change in value means your equity is now up to 20%. Simply call your mortgage company and request that your home be reappraised as it is undervalued. If your lender will not cooperate, perhaps another lender will!

> You can also get your home reappraised to see if the change in value means your equity is now up to 20%.

The bank is supposed to automatically stop taking PMI when you have reached 22% equity in your house. It does not mean that they will. You need to pay attention and give them a call. For a mortgage balance of $200,000, you could pay more than $1,000 a year in PMI! Make the call and keep that $1,000 for yourself.

Refinance

This simple method can mean easy money back to you. The best way to show this is through an easily imagined scenario. Let's take Ed and Sue. They bought their home five years ago for $300,000, with a variable rate mortgage. Their original monthly mortgage payment was $2,500. Five years have passed, and their interest rate has gone up… and so has their principal. They are now paying $3,100 per month, and their balance is $315,000.

Ed and Sue are able to keep paying the $3,100, the amount of the monthly payment they are currently paying now. However, they should shop around and refinance the mortgage to a fixed rate. The rate they have now is astronomical. The lower rate at the beginning of the mortgage is long gone and they are now paying as high as 9%.

Ed and Sue can find a fixed rate mortgage for 4% or 5%. As we have seen, that'll make a remarkable reduction in the amount of interest being paid.

> Saving on interest is like saving money over and over again.

By losing the old variable rate loan and switching to a new fixed rate loan, their principal will not go up, their balance will not go up, and their monthly payments will not go up. They will continue to make the same monthly payment, as always, and now they will pay off their home much, much faster.

Another way to bring the payment down, for a first-time mortgage or a refinance, is to put as much as possible in for the down payment. I understand that's a hard thing to do, so this is a prime opportunity to ask your family for help. Any money they can loan you will save you a ton of interest. The larger your down payment, obviously, the less you have to borrow, plus you qualify for a better interest rate.

Saving on interest is like saving money over and over again; better in your wallet than the banks.

When you look at your house, see it for the asset that it is. It can be a great source for Free Money.

CHAPTER 17

Grants

Entire books could be and have been written about grants. Grants are a glorious source of Free Money. You are given money that you never have to pay back. The government gives out millions of dollars of grants. Make that billions.

As of June 30, 2011, more than $61 billion remained to be awarded for "Contracts, Grants and Loans" from the American Recovery and Reinvestment Act of 2009!

A grant is sort of like a gift, money that is yours with no repayment, but since you have to apply for it, it's not exactly the same. I doubt your parents ever told you that your birthday was coming up and if you wanted a birthday present, you better get your application in.

I love grants also because it's Free Money from the federal government and that has a special zing for me.

As you will see, there are grants for just about everything. Personal needs, business needs, go to school, start a small business, fix up your house, travel abroad and on and on. The list is endless.

No Credit Required

One of the remarkable things with grants (besides the fact that it is money given to you that you never have to pay back) is that grants are not based on credit scores or credit history or any of that stuff that makes us all nervous.

A lot of people have bad credit. It doesn't mean a thing to the grant people. Credit scores try to measure your ability to repay a loan. Grants are not loans, so the grant givers don't care if you are able to repay because the money is yours to keep!

> Grant applications do not ask about your credit.

So if you're worried about your credit score (read *Debt Cures* for all the help you need there), worry no more. Grant applications do not ask about your credit.

Another wonderful thing about grants is that you don't have to stop at one. You can apply for as many grants as you want.

No Income Restrictions

Perhaps you're thinking that you have to be "poor" in order to qualify for a grant. That's not the case. Grants and funds from the government are not always "need based." There are many grants that have no consideration at all for income level. Lots of the rich and famous people have received grants and government money. Even George W. Bush, before he was president, received money for his baseball team's new stadium.

We sifted through the rumors and the facts, as is always the case with sports, politics and high profile types. We learned that when Mr. Bush was part of the ownership team of the Texas Rangers, the team needed a new facility and the owners talked about moving the team. To keep the franchise there, the city of Arlington gave $135 million towards the cost of building the new stadium. Mr. Bush and his fellow owners (all of them millionaires) did not repay this whopping contribution to their cause.

Is this a typical everyday scenario? Of course not, but it simply shows that grant money can flow into your hands, too.

Government grants come from federal, state, and local branches. Private grants come from companies and foundations. And, because many people don't know about these grants, or they assume that they would not qualify, a lot of this money is going unclaimed.

As I explained earlier in this book, when bills are passed in Congress, the boys in Washington throw in a little something for their pet projects, like education, women business owners, farmers, etc. That is how money from the government gets set aside for grants. It's there and cannot be repurposed somewhere else.

Private foundations also give away funding to keep their non-profit status and tax-exempt status. They are set up as a foundation and have to give away a certain percentage of their assets. Foundations can determine any cause for their grants. That is why there are so many different—and unique—opportunities.

If you are a banjo-playing scientist looking for a grant to study the mating habits of caterpillars, there very well could be a grant out there for you. Obviously, I made that up, but you get my point. Private foundations can give money to whomever and for whatever cause they see fitting their mission.

Be it government or private, there is money sitting there… just waiting for you.

Nothing Out of Pocket

With grants, there is no up-front money for you to dish out. You fill out an application—we will get to the nitty gritty later—and they let you know if you will be awarded the grant. For just about all grants, there is no processing fee or application fee, so you have nothing to lose. If the grant is charging you to apply, take a second look at it. There are all kinds of scams out there. Maybe a processing fee could run fifty bucks, but if you have to pay anything more, I would think red flag and let that one go.

Maybe you're a little familiar with grants, but have been too overwhelmed by the sheer magnitude. I understand. It would be great if there was one big clearing house for all the grants available and all you had to do was submit one application. A magic elf would sift through all the possibilities and let you know for which one you qualify.

It doesn't work that way in real life. There is not one government office in charge of all grants. All the individual agencies manage their own grant programs. That means you have to apply to each separate agency.

And, that is where some people get overwhelmed. They don't know where to begin. I'm playing the part of the magic elf to help you get started. This is where you begin. Right here, right now.

The categories are endless. What do you want money for? Give it a Google search and see what you can find. Let me show some possibilities.

College students who qualify may be able to get a grant of up to $4,000 per year to pay their bills. Contact: www2.ed.gov/about/offices/list/fsa/index.html for federal student aid. Want to learn a foreign language? Get a fellowship grant to pay your tuition.

Contact: www2.ed.gov/about/offices/list/ope/iegps/index.html for the office of postsecondary education. You can get a grant for $28,000 to get your doctorate degree overseas and not have to repay it. Contact: www2.ed.gov/programs/iegpsirs/index.html for international research and studies program. There are hundreds of grants to help you go to school! Contact your school or state aid office or go to: www.studentaid.ed.gov to get Free Money for your higher education.

Have you finished your degree and want to continue? Many grants and fellowships are available. See: www.aauw.org/what-we-do/educational-funding-and-awards/; www.grants.gov; or look up grants in your field. Opportunities abound. For example, the National Institute of Health offers programs for medical and dental students (http://grants.nih.gov/grants/oer.htm). You can also check out the Department of Education at: http://www2.ed.gov/about/offices/list/ocfo/grants/grants.html for grant information.

> All the individual agencies manage their own grant programs. That means you have to apply to each separate agency.

We're only just getting started. Once you start playing around online, you will see how many possibilities are out there. Personal grants, government grants, green grants, health grants, state grants, travel grants, college grants, business grants, minority grants, low income grants, teaching grants, nursing grants, and on and on.

You know where your interest is and what you need to search for. Just follow the guidelines and apply.

Where do you want to start?

Buying a Home

There are dozens and dozens of programs for home assistance, especially if you are a first time homebuyer. Try this site:

www.first-time-homebuyer-site.com/?f.

You can also find your state immediately by doing a Google search with "First Time Home Buyer Program" and the name of your state.

It can be overwhelming with all the options out there. For example:

Texas offers a grant equal to 5% of the mortgage on the home—Texas Department of Housing and Community Affairs. See www.tdhca.state.tx.us/homeownership/fthb/buyer_intro.htm if you're thinking about building a home. Texas also has tax credits (gotta love those tax credits!) for mortgages—Texas Mortgage Credit Program. See www.tdhca.state.tx.us/homeownership/fthb for more information.

Kentucky has a Down Payment Assistance Program. Visit http://www.kyhousing.org/page.aspx?id=297 for information on down payment and closing cost assistance. California has a variety of programs; like the California Homebuyers Down Payment Assistance Programs (CHDAP). See www.calhfa.ca.gov/homebuyer/ if you're a first time homebuyer. Minnesota has its share of programs, too. Visit http://firstbuyerprograms.com/minnesota-first-time-home-buyer-grants/ for first time homebuyer grants, programs and loans. Iowa offers up to $2,500 in assistance for down payment or closing costs. Visit the Iowa Finance Authority at www.iowafinanceauthority.gov/Home/Index?aspxerrorpath=/en/for_home_buyers/ to learn more about their home ownership program.

Also, look into the FHA (Federal Housing Authority) for programs. (www.fha.com/fha_programs). The site www.FHA.com has links to programs such as AmeriDream, which offers grants for down payments and closing costs for up to 10% of the purchase price of the home; and The Nehemiah Program, which provides down payment assistance; and American Family Funds, which also helps with down payments and closing costs.

The above is just a sampling. Closing costs? You can get them paid. Need help with the down payment? You can get money for that. Repairs and rehab? You can get funds for that, too.

Every state has mortgage programs. Click on www.cc-bc.com/state_grants.html and see what your state has to offer.

There are homeowner assistance programs that are not just for first-time buyers. People who need emergency help with the house payment can find aid. Google "Homeowners Emergency Assistance Programs" and the name of your state.

For example, states like Pennsylvania grant loans up to $60,000. See www.phfa.org/consumers/homeowners/hemap.aspx. The city of Minneapolis has grants of $10,000 ($1.5 million available). Cities like Minneapolis also offer housing loans. Visit http://www.minneapolismn.gov/cped/housing/cped_city_living to see what's available.

Many real estate firms offer information on state programs. See http://www.minnesotafirsttimehomebuyer.com/minnesota-programs.php for a list of local Minnesota programs and contact numbers.

Even if you don't live in Minnesota, you can see just how many resources might be available to you in your home state!

ALL of these sites have all the details you will need to know, like any income limits, how to apply and phone numbers to call with questions. There is a WEALTH of homebuyer and homeowner assistance programs out there! Your Free Money is waiting.

Energy

How about a little energy boost? There are programs available in every state. Need help to pay the heating bills in winter? It's available. There are summer programs, too. If you're in need, there could be Free Money to help you out.

The LIHEAP (Low Income Heating Energy Assistance Program) has links to all state programs at www.liheap.ncat.org/. When the heating bills go up, it's nice to know there is assistance for those who need it.

> There are programs available in every state.

For example, in Massachusetts (http://www.liheap.ncat.org/), there is a discount of 20-40% on utility bills plus a 5% senior citizen discount. Free services are also available to make homes more energy efficient.

Things like wall insulation, attic insulation, air sealing, and heating system replacement is provided by these programs.

More residential energy support programs are available through APS. See www.aps.com for its list of services.

How about discounts on phone service? There are programs that offer that, too. Visit www.fcc.gov/lifeline to see if you qualify.

Child Safety

How about free child car seats?

There are different programs in different communities. Call your local United Way office, local police department or check with your hospital or insurance company. Some states have programs that "rent" car seats for five dollars.

Visit the National Highway Traffic Safety Administration (NHTSA)— www.nhtsa.gov/ —for info on safety seats and how to properly secure your child.

Job Search

How about getting a job? Many people lost their jobs in this strained economy. Think about your career plans. Think about education. If you have a desire to teach, now is a wonderful opportunity. Even if you are not exactly a traditional age student, you can go back and get your degree. Teachers with a little life experience are scholarship eligible, too.

Another huge need is in the field of nursing. Scholarship money is ready and waiting for you to apply for it. A severe nursing shortage is on the horizon. Most nurses get to pick their schedules and their pay is great; usually full-time pay for less than full-time hours.

According to the U.S. Department of Labor, health care occupations are projected to create millions of new job openings, including:

✔ Medical Assistants

✔ Health Information Technologists

✔ Medical Coding & Billing Specialists

✔ Medical Record Transcriptionists

✔ Registered Nurses (RN)... more than 600,000 needed, and the number of online nursing programs continues to rise

Think about getting your nursing degree online and schedule your work hours around your family. That's a win-win!

Volunteering

You can volunteer and get paid for it.

Go to www.seniorcorps.org to see how seniors are helping America and getting paid for it. Some volunteers can earn an hourly tax-free stipend. You can also receive accidental and liability insurance while doing your volunteer duties. That's something to get excited about! A stipend for getting paid for something you love to do.

Look up Volunteers of America. You can get $200 per month. And, paid time off and holidays. Visit www.voa.org to find your local office.

Does the role of foster grandparent appeal to you? If you are age 60 or over and want to spend time with children, this is a way to do something you love, a way to give back to a child and get some Free Money for you.

You can spend time with a child, change that child's life, and ultimately change yours as well. Foster grandparents give a few hours a week to tutor a child and help with reading. You are, in essence, giving love and support, the main role of grandparents. You can do this for up to 40 hours per week and get paid.

According to www.nationalservice.gov/programs/senior-corps, people who volunteer live longer and have a positive outlook on life. Is that you?

For more information on volunteer programs that provide volunteer stipends, plus meals, transportation, insurance, an annual physical exam, a uniform if needed and recognition activities; view the Seniorcorps web site, Volunteers of America and the Resource Center at www.nationalservice.gov/programs/senior-corps/foster-grandparents or call 800-860-2684.

Savings Matching

The state of New York has launched a special savings plan for low income New Yorkers called $aveNYC Accounts. The city matches a portion of the tax refund that the resident deposits into this account. It encourages savings and the match is FREE MONEY.

For more info, go to www.nyc.gov/html/dca/html/resources/resources.shtml. Many other states offer similar, unique programs.

Search and Find

Searching for grants can be like being a kid in a candy store. There is so much to choose from, with some amazing resources online for finding and applying for grants:

Try www.govengine.com. This site is enormous. It's the monster of government sites. So much information, it boggles the brain. Use it to guide you to all state agency information and national as well.

When I say it's overwhelming, it's because there's so much to sift through; I'm not kidding. That's why I am telling you how to use someone else who has already done the sifting. Try http://foundationcenter.org/.

On this site, you're able to search four complete databases: Grant makers, Companies, Grants and 990s. Check it out to retrieve the latest facts on more than 96,000 funders and 1.5 million grants.

To search the database for nonprofit organizations in the US, try www.guidestar.com. There are close to 1.8 million nonprofits in our country. And, many of those give grants and low cost loans.

Government Benefits

First, you have to check out www.benefits.gov. This site has information on thousands of programs. It's easy to navigate. There are two ways to maneuver this site. Let's assume you have no idea what you might qualify for or what you are looking for specifically. Click on the "Start Here" button. It will take you to an easy-to-answer questionnaire.

> The questions are simple and straightforward, and completely anonymous.

There are some questions to go through and depending upon how fast you read, it will take you 5 to 10 minutes to complete. The questions are simple and straightforward and completely anonymous. You don't give your name or social security number. The only personal questions are age, gender and income level. After you answer the questions, a list of possible grant or benefit programs pops up for which you could be eligible.

If you already know where your interest lies, for example, "utilities" or "education," you can also use the Quick Search feature on govbenefits.gov. Select the topics, which include: Awards; Counseling; Disaster Relief; Financial Assistance; Grants; Scholarships; Fellowships; Housing; Loans; Social Security/

Pension; Child Care; Disability Assistance; Education; Food; Health Care; Insurance; Medicare; and Utilities. A list of all the programs in that category appears.

Click each one that interests you or that's in your state. Then you can view the details of each, or click to see if you could be eligible. You answer a few questions, and what you may be eligible for is narrowed down. Some of the Free Money sources are limited to your income level, but even if you have a high income, there are still low-cost loan opportunities on this site.

www.grants.gov

Another fantastic resource that is not widely known or publicized is www.grants.gov.

You can review the list of agencies and programs that you have pre-qualified for based upon the answers to your questions. This feature alone can save you days and weeks, if not months and years, of time searching for possible Free Money sources.

Most federal agencies that offer grants post them here. You can read about the grant, see if you qualify and download and submit your application… all online. Instead of having to search through hundreds of different agency programs, this site allows you to look for what you may be able to apply for, all in one location. There are hundreds of grant programs from many agencies on this site and billions of dollars to be awarded!

With www.grants.gov, the search process is brought into one big site where you enter your information just once. You can look at grants by agency name or by category.

You can become aware of grants and sources that you never knew about. If you just want to browse through the grants, you don't have to register. If you want to apply for a grant, you will need to register. Just follow the instructions on the web site and you'll be on your way to Free Money.

SBA

There are also many programs through the Small Business Administration that you should not overlook. These are not all grants, but loans with very good interest rates and easy terms.

Don't overlook all the foundations and private sources that provide various funds. See: www.foundationcenter.org/getstarted/individuals/ or www.fundsnetservices.com. There are thousands of possibilities at your fingertips.

The official web site of the federal government, USA.gov (www.usa.gov), contains valuable information about all US government agencies. The first topic listed is Benefits and Grants. This link gives you lots of official information on grants, loans, financial aid and other benefits from the US government. You can even sign up to be notified when the benefit page is updated.

Govloans.gov (www.govloans.gov) is your gateway to government loan information. This site directs you to the loan information that best meets your needs and is an excellent source for locating loans for children, agriculture, business, disaster relief, education, housing, veterans or just about anything for which you might need a loan.

The Small Business Administration has implemented programs that have drastically changed the futures of the individuals and the companies that have qualified for them.

There's the Small Business Innovation Research program, also known as the SBIR. In an effort to stimulate the forward-thinking aspects of qualifying small businesses, the SBIR offers a host of monetary awards, some totaling as much as $100,000. Visit http://archive.sba.gov/aboutsba/sbaprograms/sbir/index.html to learn about programs that can find Free Money… or money that's almost free.

The SBA Office of Technology also has the Small Business Technology Transfer Program (STTR). Five federal departments award $2 billion to small high-tech businesses in this program. If that's your business and you have fewer than 500 employees, you can apply to get a piece of that $2 billion pie. The Small Business Administration offers other great Free Money programs, and you can learn more about them at www.sba.gov. I can't begin to list everything, but I hope you get the idea that the money is there, and I hope you see that finding it isn't as hard as you may have thought.

Some Federal money programs, grants, and loans:

- ✔ $25,000 "micro-loan" to start a business—www.sba.gov

- ✔ $200,000 to run a ranch or a farm—www.fsa.usda.gov

- ✔ $200,000 credit line for small businesses— http://www.sba.gov/category/navigation-structure/loans-grants/small-business-loans/sba-loan-programs

- ✔ $500,000 to start a business—www.sba.gov

- ✔ $300,000 to help you get government contracts— www.dla.mil/SmallBusiness/Pages/default.aspx

- ✔ $500,000 for females and minorities to get government contracts— www.dot.gov/osdbu/

In addition to grants, there are many loans available that are quick and guaranteed by the Small Business Administration. There are Small Business Development Centers in every state as well. Contact: www.sba.gov/content/small-business-development-centers-sbdcs to find yours.

Need some start-up money to get things going? Go to: www.sba.gov/about-offices-content/1/2890. The SBIC funding for small businesses includes $10 billion from the government and private funding of more than $12 billion.

The SBIC site likes to share their success stories and reading them is very inspirational. Check out: http://archive.sba.gov/aboutsba/sbaprograms/inv/INV_SUCCESS_STORIES.html and see if you are in awe, as I was. They state it perfectly, "The most exciting potential of an SBIC investment is how it can turn one small company into a great success story."

Your company could join the ranks of big names (who once were small) like America Online, Apple Computer, Federal Express, Gymboree, Jenny Craig, Inc., Staples and many more. There is Free Money for your business. Who knows, you could be "small potatoes" today, and in the future, you could join the list that contains the likes of Outback Steakhouse, Restoration Hardware and Costco.

> There are hundreds of state agencies with money to help your business.

There are hundreds of state agencies with money to help your business. Let's take a state like New York. Growing a business in New York can be tough, especially when it's technology-based. With all the fierce competition out there, it can be daunting for a business owner who hopes to transform the market with cutting-edge technologies. That is exactly why the Small Business Technology Investment Fund Program (SBTIF) exists.

Free Money can change everything. Watch your business soar to heights you never imagined, all because of the venture capital you gained from the SBTIF. New York's economic development agency, Empire State Development, started this fund with the hope of nurturing all businesses based in technology.

In a place like Rhode Island, Workforce Development is of great value. The Governor's Workforce Board knows just how important it is for employees of any business to possess the best skills and techniques. Great employees build great companies; it's a fact.

That's why the Governor's Workforce offers a series of grants to develop and train a team that will yield your business the best possible results. These Comprehensive Worker Training Grants can get you up to $50,000 of Free Money! If a stronger workforce is what your company needs, then this grant will be of tremendous benefit. Learn more about it here: www.rihric.com/grants.htm.

Women Business Owners

The entire purpose of the Small Business Association's Office of Women's Business Ownership is to help women achieve their dreams and improve their communities by providing assistance for starting a business. They provide training on how to get started and how to maintain a successful business. They offer plenty of help along the way. Check out the SBA's web site for all the details [www.sba.gov/about-offices-content/1/2895].

Another wonderful resource for women is SBA's Women Business Centers (WBC). With the ability to guide you every step of the way, this SBA program provides resource centers all across the nation to help women get their businesses launched.

Grants are available to these WBCs for five years, and there is even an option to renew for another five years. The program's mission is to "level the playing field." The WBC provides assistance to new businesses and existing businesses looking to expand.

There are also business grants available through the Women's Financial Fund (http://www.womensbusinessgrants.com/who.shtml).

Educators

This site— http://www.k12grants.org/grant_opps.htm —is dubbed as "your one stop site for PK–12 school grant opportunities." It's a real A+ site for educators. They offer grant writing tips and workshops focused solely on how to write successful grants in the area of education. In addition to help in writing grant applications, they provide a list of grants and where to find more information and opportunities. If education is your field, this is your site.

At www.foundations.org, someone else has done the searching for you and compiled a directory of charitable foundations. They've gathered the information; you simply click away. Select "Directories" and choose either "community foundations" or "corporate/private foundations." A long list of people/organizations giving away Free Money pops up for you to peruse. You can then select from your area of interest/locale or a certain corporation.

Simply finding what's available is more than half the battle in the search for Free Money. Sites like this get you on your way quicker, and it is so easy! If you are looking for scholarships, check out all the community foundations in your state, county and city. They usually have many private donors offering a wide variety of private scholarships.

Ten minutes spent searching these sites could land you $10,000 or more. That's definitely a wise investment of time and a wonderful investment in your future… or the future of your student.

Grant Solutions

Another site to add to your favorites: https://home.grantsolutions.gov/home/. This is the web address for the Grants Center of Excellence (COE). It's a partnership between agencies within Health and Human Services, the Department of Agriculture, the Denali Commission and the Department of the Treasury. The COE states that these partner agencies distribute more than $250 billion in grants each year.

The CFDA, Catalog of Federal Domestic Assistance, is also a great resource. This site gives access to a database of all federal programs that are available to state and local governments. You can search and find what you're eligible for and then contact the agency or program to apply. The site is updated biweekly as new programs are posted by federal agencies. See: http://www.grantmoneyarticles.com/assistance.html.

Another opportunity is a loan program of up to $10,000 for women in business (www.count-me-in.org). You can also check out:

- ✔ http://staff.lib.msu.edu/harris23/grants/3women.htm
- ✔ www.fundsnetservices.com/searchresult/15/Women-Grants.html
- ✔ www.womensnet.net

There are also a host of others.

Another helpful resource, www.ehomebasedbusiness.com/articles, provides a list of 25 important telephone numbers for those launching a business.

Education

There are many grants available for college tuition and expenses. If you need help finding a school that's right for you, the fastest and easiest web tools are www.fastweb.com and www.education-connection.com. They are free services to get students matched up with colleges that serve them and their needs.

There is money for online degrees now, too. Just so you know, online degrees don't state that they are online, so future employers won't know if you went to school at a traditional campus or attended online from home. There are 3.5 million people who earn degrees online now and employers give them the same respect as "normal" degrees.

Be aware that if you are pursuing an education later in life and want to go back to school, many schools offer the option of writing about your life experience. This "experiential learning portfolio" can equate to college credit that you don't have to pay for.

Remember to apply for scholarships, no matter your age. The scholarship money depends on the source. They may look at your grades, your need, your religion, your heritage or your major. There are many factors.

> The scholarship money depends on the source.

If you are military, you can use veteran's benefits to pay for school. Go to www.military.com for a list of schools. For this to apply to your situation, you must be separated from active duty for less than ten years. If you are still on active duty, you can use your military benefits TA Awards.

A great source for regular education grants is www.school-grantsblog.com. They break down the top twenty most popular grants. They include Pell Grants, Federal Supplemental Educational Opportunity Grant (FSEOG), SMART Grants, Academic Competitiveness Grant, TEACH Grants, GPA Isn't Everything Scholarship, SuperCollege Scholarship, Sallie Mae, ODS, Best Buy Scholarships and Dell Foundation Scholarships.

Simply go to www.schoolgrantsblog.com and click on the 20 popular grants tab and then click on the name of the grant or scholarship to take you to the application page. I love when it's that easy.

Travel

Want to travel, see the world or study abroad? There are ways to do it without having to pay. Try:

- ✔ www.passportintime.com
- ✔ www2.ed.gov/programs/iegpsflasf/index.html
- ✔ www.nsep.gov/initiatives/

These sites will give you information on scholarships and fellowships that provide significant funding for study abroad, in the amounts of up to $20,000 and even $30,000. You can use these funds to study abroad or in the United States.

The National Security Education Programs funds Boren Fellowships, which provide grad students the opportunity to study languages and cultures that are deemed important to US national security. Students who desire a career in the federal government and wish to take coursework abroad should consider this opportunity. Fellowships are up to $30,000. Applications must be completed online. See: www.iie.org.

Have you finished your degree and want to continue? Many grants and fellowships are available. See:

- ✔ www.aauw.org/what-we-do/educational-funding-and-awards/
- ✔ www.grants.gov

You can also look up grants in your field. Opportunities abound. For example, the National Institute of Health offers programs for medical and dental students (grants.nih.gov/grants/oer.htm). You can also check out the Department of Education at: www2.ed.gov/about/offices/list/ocfo/grants/grants.html. There are also many private funding sources out there. One such program offers fellowships and grants for education research (www.spencer.org). Private foundations are a wonderfully smart source for Free Money.

For the Federal Government Agency Directory, you can contact: http://publications.usa.gov/or call 1-800-FED-INFO.

This is just scratching the surface of all the grants that are out there. The idea here is to turn you on to the option of grants, not list every single grant opportunity. You have the Internet as your tool. This book is the light pointing you in the right direction.

Depending upon your vocation or your need, you could get grants from multiple sources. Think of researchers who rely on grant money to do their work. A lot of that funding comes from private sources. Individuals and corporations set up foundations as a philanthropic entity or to support a cause, such as a memorial to a loved one.

Private foundations are another great source for Free Money. Entire books are devoted to that topic as well. We devoted the next chapter.

CHAPTER 18

Foundations

Besides grants that come from government entities, there are many private foundations that give Free Money as well.

The sizes of the foundations, the amount of money they disburse, and the reasons for doing so are different. There's no one size fits all... or one foundation fits all.

Giving Back

Many wealthy people, like Bill Gates, start foundations. Celebrities and athletes do, too. And, so do many folks who aren't as famous.

CNN once reported the story of Dr. Benjamin Carson, a doctor and director of pediatric neurosurgery at Johns Hopkins Children's Center. Dr. Carson is called an unlikely hero. His autobiography and TV movie of his life are titled Gifted Hands.

His is the story of a young boy with a troubled past who grows up and becomes a doctor. How troubled was his past? He stabbed a schoolmate (saved by a belt buckle of all things) and he went after his mother with a hammer (his brother was able to restrain him). He had a terrible violent temper and yet was able to overcome it.

Dr. Benjamin Carson overcame much adversity in his life and achieved top standing in his field. He was also awarded the Presidential Medal of Freedom in 2008, the highest award a civilian can receive in our country. Dr. Carson and his wife created a private foundation to provide college scholarships for those students with academic excellence and humanitarian qualities.

> They give funding to others who are contributing to make this world a little better.

One grateful recipient of the Carson Scholars Fund stated, "I probably should not be where I am. I went to Baltimore public schools. My father's in jail; my mother is dead. Statistically, I should not be here. I should be on parole somewhere or even dead. I never looked at it that way. I made it through."

This student read Dr. Carson's autobiography, and said that it was "a relief to see someone who grew up in the city and didn't have a luxurious life, but overcame it all." I love stories about underdogs, those who overcome adversity and do something.

Many times, foundations are started by those who want to give back. They give funding to others who are contributing to make this world a little better.

There are many foundations, started by many different folks, for many different reasons. And the criteria vary as well. Want a sample of foundations? Here are just some of the foundations that give personal and business grants:

- ✔ Wheless Foundation, P.O. Box 1119, Shreveport, LA 71152

- ✔ Simon & Schwab Foundation, P.O. Box 1014, Columbus, GA 31902

✔ Coulter Foundation, P.O. Box 5247, Denver, CO 80217

✔ Thatcher Foundation, P.O. Box 1401, Pueblo, CO 81002

✔ Biddle Foundation, Inc., 61 Broadway, Room 2912, New York, NY 10006

✔ Avery-Fuller Children Center, 251 Kearney Street, No. 301, San Francisco, CA 94108

✔ Jane Nugent Cochems Trust, c/o Colorado National Bank of Denver, P.O. Box 5168, Denver, CO 80217

✔ Unocal Foundation, P.O. Box 7600, Los Angeles, CA 90051

✔ Wal-Mart Foundation, 702 Southwest 8th Street, Bentonville, AK 72716

✔ The Piton Foundation, 511 16th Street, Suite 700, Denver, CO 80202

✔ Frank R. Seaver Trust, 714 W. Olympic Boulevard, Los Angeles, CA 90015

✔ Earl B. Gilmore Foundation, 160 S. Fairfax Avenue, Los Angeles, CA 90036

✔ The Commonwealth Fund, One East 75th Street, New York, NY 10021-2692

✔ The Cullen Foundation, P.O. Box 1600, Houston, TX 77251

✔ The James Irvine Foundation, One Market Plaza, San Francisco, CA 94105

✔ William Penn Foundation, 1630 Locust Street, Philadelphia, PA 19103

✔ Blanchard Foundation, c/o Boston Sake, One Boston Place, Boston, MA 02106

✔ Xerox Foundation, P.O. Box 1600, Stamford, CT 06904

✔ Fairchild Industries, 20301 Century Boulevard, Germantown, MD 20874

✔ Charles and Els Bendheim Foundation, One Parker Plaza, Fort Lee, NJ 07024

✔ Blue Horizon Health & Welfare Trust, c/o Reid & Reige, Lakeville, CT 06039

✔ Broadcasters Foundation, Inc., 320 West 57th Street, New York, NY 10019

✔ Copley Fund, P.O. Box 696, Morrisville, VT 05661

✔ The Hawaii Foundation, 111 South King Street, P.O. Box 3170, Honolulu, HI 96802

✔ Inland Steel-Ryerson Foundation, 30 West Monroe Street, Chicago, IL 60603

✔ Northern Indiana Giving Program, 5265 Hohman Avenue, Hammond, IN 46320

✔ Cambridge Foundation, 99 Bishop Allan Drive, Cambridge, MA 02139

✔ Barker Foundation, P.O. Box 328, Nashua, NH 03301

✔ Morris Joseloff Foundation, Inc., 125 La Salee Rd, W. Hartford, CT 06107

✔ Deposit Guaranty Foundation, P.O. Box 1200, Jackson, MS 39201

✔ Haskin Foundation, 200 E. Broadway, Louisville, KY 40202

✔ The Dayton Foundation, 1395 Winters Bank Tower, Dayton, OH 45423

✔ Ford Motor Company, The American Road, Dearborn, MI 48121

✔ Bohen Foundation, 1716 Locust Street, Des Moines, IA 50303

✔ Yonkers Charitable Trust, 701 Walnut Street, Des Moines, IA 50306

✔ Miles Foundation, P.O. Box 40, Elkhart, IN 46515

✔ Ametek Foundation, 410 Park Avenue, New York, NY 10022

✔ Horace B. Packer Foundation, 61 Main Street, Wellsboro, PA 16901

✔ John B. Lynch Scholarship Fund, P.O. Box 4248, Wilmington, DE 19807

✔ Camden Home for Senior Citizens, 66 Washington Street, Camden, ME 04843

✔ The Clark Foundation, 30 Wall Street, New York, NY 10005

✔ Richard & Helen DeVos Foundation, 7154 Windy Hill, SE, Grand Rapids, MI 49506

✔ Muskegon County Foundation, Fraunthal Center, Suite 304, 407 W. Western Avenue, Muskegon, MI 49440

✔ The H&R Block Foundation, 4410 Main Street, Kansas City, MO 64111

✔ New Hampshire Fund, One South Street, P.O. Box 1335, Concord, NH 03302-1335

✔ The Shearwater Foundation, Inc., c/o Alexander Nixon, 423 West 43rd Street, New York, NY 10036

Here is a list of foundations that give grants for medical assistance, welfare assistance, financial help for needy people, and financial help for educational use:

✔ The Fasken Foundation, 500 West Texas Avenue, Suite 1160, Midland, TX, 79701

✔ The Rosario Foundation, 100 Broadway Avenue, Carnegie, PA 15106-2421

✔ Orange Memorial Hospital Corporation, P.O. Box 396, Orange, TX 77630

✔ The Perpetual Benevolent Fund, c/o Bay Bank Middlesex, 300 Washington St., Newton, MA, 02158

✔ The Bagby Foundation for Musical Arts, 501 5th Ave., New York, NY 10017

✔ Larabee Fund Association, c/o Connecticut National Bank, 777 Main St., Hartford, CT 06115

✔ Battistone Foundation, P.O. Box 3858, Santa Barbara, CA 93103

✔ Avery-Fuller Children Center, 251 Kearney St., San Francisco, CA 94108

✔ Vero Beach Foundation for the Elderly, c/o First National Bank, 255 S. County Road, Palm Beach, FL, 33480

✔ Smock Foundation, c/o Lincoln National Bank and Trust Co., P.O. Box 960, Fort Wayne, IN 46801

✔ Glifilin Memorial, Inc., W-555 First National Bank Building, St. Paul, MN, 55101

✔ Clarke Testamentary Trust/Fund Foundation, US National Bank of Oregon, P.O. Box 3168, Portland, OR, 97208

✔ Welsh Trust, P.O. Box 244, Walla Walla, WA 99362

(Source: members.tripod.com/promo_info/free/freecashgrants. htm)

Many corporations give grants. To find more information on corporate giving, visit www.grantspace.org/Tools/Knowledge-Base/Funding-Resources/Corporations/corporate-giving.

Foundation Directory

Foundation Directory Online, available on a subscription basis, allows you to perform online searches on nearly 100,000 foundations, corporate givers, and grant-making public charities.

Use the terms "Company-sponsored foundation" or "Corporate giving program" from the "Type of Grant maker" index to find corporate funders. Corporate Giving Online, also available as a subscription database, provides access to close to 4,300 company-sponsored foundations and corporate-giving programs (the same grant makers are included in the above-mentioned Foundation Directory Online).

It also provides searchable profiles for more than 3,600 companies with facts about business type, names and affiliations of officers and directors. It also lists subsidiary names and locations to help you find local divisions and offices for a parent company.

> The Internet Prospector's Reference Desk on Corporations is also a good starting point for researching companies.

Hoover's Online is a user-friendly tool for finding basic company information and news.

The Corporations/Executive Info section of David Lamb's Prospect Research Page is an excellent collection of links that may

202 | Chapter 18

prove useful in pinpointing information on a specific corporation's charitable giving interests.

Philanthropy News Digest (PND) is an online compendium of weekly news abstracts on foundations, corporate giving and grants. Use the PND Archives to search past issues of the Philanthropy News Digest archive, dating back to January of 1995.

The Foundation Center's RFP Bulletin provides listings of Requests for Proposals (RFPs). Each listing provides a brief overview of a current funding opportunity offered by corporate funders and other grant-making organizations. You can subscribe for free to an e-mail version of this weekly posting.

Application

Most foundations will have an application, form or certain requirements to apply for grants. In general, if you write a letter, a grant proposal or complete an application, you need to write to the point and be brief. Don't use flowery words and don't ask for more than one grant per letter.

Foundations in general want to know:

A. Your plan.

B. State your needs.

C. Describe the individual or organization requesting the grant.

D. The financial potentials of your plan.

E. List supporters.

F. The total cost of your plan.

G. Describe how your needs will be met with their grant.

The foundation wants to see that their dollars will be wisely spent and help someone further their educational goals, artistic goals, business goals, etc.

Remember, there are all kinds of grants for all kinds of purposes.

For example, let's look at the Bagby Foundation for Musical Arts. This foundation offers grants for those completing their graduate studies who need additional specific coaching lessons to make their professional debut.

Those music students interested in this grant are required to write a short letter explaining the financial need and their talent. The grant is a 3-6 month musical study grant for promising young opera singers and classical musicians based on talent and need.

So, if you know any young opera singers or classical musicians, let them know about the Bagby Foundation. The address is listed above in the list of education grants. The Bagby Foundation also offers several grants per year to elderly musicians.

The name "Perpetual Benevolent Fund" captured my attention. What does this foundation do? They support local area residents in need. Even a washing machine or refrigerator is an acceptable request for their aid. People helping people… the only thing better than Free Money.

You may have heard that some foundations give grant awards only to nonprofit organizations. That's true, but many foundations give directly to individuals, like the Bagby Foundation and the Perpetual Benevolent folks.

What Are You Looking For?

Don't listen to the naysayers who say "normal people" cannot get grants. There are funders who support individuals, for:

- ✔ Research Scholarships
- ✔ Student Loans
- ✔ Fellowships
- ✔ Internships
- ✔ Residencies
- ✔ Book Authorship
- ✔ Schoolteacher Contests
- ✔ Artistic Works... and on and on.

Many libraries carry the publication *Foundation Grants for Individuals*, by the Foundation Center. Check your local library.

Ask around in your local community. You may be surprised to find grant opportunities in your own backyard. Check in your town through local social service agencies, professional societies, trade consortiums, community foundations, United Way offices, churches, art councils, civic clubs or Chambers of Commerce.

Here's where you can find examples of successful grant proposals: http://foundationcenter.org/getstarted/tutorials/gfr/proposal.html.

Don't overlook all the foundations and private sources that provide various funds. See:

- ✔ www.foundationcenter.org/getstarted/individuals/
- ✔ www.fundsnetservices.com/

The official web site of the federal government, USA.gov (http://www.usa.gov/Citizen/Topics/Benefits.shtml) contains valuable information about government benefits, grants and financial aid.

Govloans.gov (www.govloans. gov) is your gateway to government loan information. This site directs you to the loan information that best meets your needs and is an excellent source for locating loans for children, agriculture, business, disaster relief, education, housing, veterans or just about anything for which you might need a loan.

> Don't overlook all the foundations and private sources that provide various funds.

So go to your keyboard and start typing. Hundreds of Free Money possibilities are at your fingertips.

CHAPTER 19

Free Services/ Assistance

As I have explained, Free Money is also free services. Getting something for free is another way of getting more money in your pocket. You paid nothing, but received a benefit. That is Free Money.

Free services could be anything. A free haircut. That's money in your pocket. A free massage. That's money is your pocket. A free lawn mowing service. That's money in your pocket.

Anything you receive without spending a dime helps your financial situation.

If times are tough at your house, you may need to seek out free services. But whether you're budget crunched or not, free services are another way of saying Free Money. This book is all about showing you ways to obtain Free Money, from any source. No questions, no shame.

There are lots of different types of government programs out there. Let's say you've been accepted for SSI—Social Security Income payments. If you happen to live in Rhode Island, they have a bridge fund to tide you over while you're waiting. For details on this particular program, see www.dhs.ri.gov.

In fact, most states supplement the federal SSI payment, which gives you even more income each month. Payments vary depending upon your income, living arrangements and other factors. For the details, contact your state Social Security office or www.ssa.gov/ssi.

There are also programs that offer general assistance to families and they vary from state to state, and may even be different county to county. Go to www.benefits.gov to fill out a questionnaire. Based upon your answers, the web site provides links to programs for which you may qualify.

The easiest way is to go to www.benefits.gov and click on BENEFITS, then click BY STATE. Click on your state. Click on a program and it gives you all the next steps you need to do. It's a beautiful thing and easy to navigate.

We've only just begun. Buckle up. I've got a long list of services and assistance. Medical services include a number of topics in that area alone. Free legal services, too. Let's go ahead and discuss some of what's available for you. It'll also get you thinking of free services that you never thought of.

Prescriptions

If anything is out of whack in this country, it is the pharmaceutical hold on the purse strings of this nation. In fact, I wrote a whole book on that topic, too. I could go on and on about how to cure yourself naturally.

This book will show you how to get help paying for the outrageously high prescription medicines you may be taking.

Meds are a killer to any budget, especially for the elderly or anyone on a fixed budget. In fact, meds are a killer to any budget, regardless of your age or income.

The good news is that prescription help is available. Five million folks have discovered something called Partnership for Prescription Assistance. Visit www.pparx.org for the whole scoop.

In general, this service is a partnership of doctors, drug companies, health care providers and patient advocate groups. Amen to that. The Partnership for Prescription Assistance helps patients who do not have prescription benefits through insurance get the medicines they need, either through a public or private program.

Many people are now able to get their meds for free or just about free. This partnership is a one stop shopping, giving access to 475 patient assistance programs and 180 programs offered through the drug companies.

Some people are not comfortable using the Internet, so the PPA has a toll free telephone number as well: 888-477-2669.

To get qualified, you simply have to answer a few short questions. The site or the folks at PPA will guide you to a program. Forms for the programs are available for download or on the phone. If you need help filling out the form, someone from PPA will assist you. Ask them how they can also help with Medicare prescription drug coverage.

> There are no fees to use PPA and almost all of the programs offer their services free of charge.

The Partnership for Prescription Assistance helps qualifying patients get the drugs they need. The system has access to more than 2,500 medicines. The PPA helps match patients to prescription programs that provide free or nearly free medicines.

There are no fees to use PPA and almost all of the programs offer their services free of charge. There are other imitator programs out there that try to rip you off. Don't fall for it. This Partnership will not charge you.

[Source: www.pparx.org]

Besides PPA, there are many other prescription drug programs. If you don't have health insurance, or if your insurance doesn't include good prescription drug benefits, look for generic drug offers at many major supermarkets and drug stores.

You can also check these private groups that offer prescription assistance.

- ✔ HealthWell Foundation: http://healthwellfoundation.org/
- ✔ FamilyWize discount drug card: www.familywize.org/
- ✔ Needy Meds: www.needymeds.org
- ✔ Rx Hope: www.rxhope.com
- ✔ Chronic Disease Fund: www.cdfund.org/
- ✔ The Access Project: www.housingworks.org/access/pa2.html

Some states have drug assistance programs. Google "prescription programs" and the name of your state. For example, New York has a state program: applications are available at pharmacies and community organizations, online at nyprescriptionsaver.fhsc.com or by a toll-free number: 800-788-6917. Workers are eligible if they're 50 to 64 years old and making up to $35,000 a year, or married with household income of $50,000.

Odds are your state has a prescription program.

Mental Health Medical Benefits

With the state of the economy, high rates of unemployment, people losing their homes, plus the ever-present issues of death, divorce and disease, more and more people are struggling with depression and other issues that can lead to more serious health problems.

If you can get help early on, the better off you—and your family—will be. There is a web site called freementalhealth.com. And, it offers exactly what it says. Many times people put off going to the doctor because money is tight and they think they should spend it on other things. And when it comes to emotional or mental health issues, we sometimes think we can handle it on our own.

Now you know that free help is out there. Take advantage of it. Use this web site to find what you need. The site is free and confidential.

If drugs or alcohol are a problem, there are free programs in many communities. You can use a local directory or use freementalhealth. com to find 24,000 locations for free clinics and drug rehab programs.

According to the site, it was set up so that you can type in anywhere in the US to find out what drug or mental health treatment is available for free. Drugs, depression, anxiety, bipolar, schizophrenia. Also, free help for children with autism, depression, anxiety, ADD or ADHD.

Kids' Health Care

There are programs that allow children to be eligible for free health insurance. See www.insurekidsnow.gov. Every state has its own rules. It can pay for doctor and dentist visits, meds and hospital care. Call 1-800-KIDS-NOW for info on your state.

Teenagers are covered too. A message to all working parents; these programs are for you! Filling out a short application form is all you need to do.

The Office of Family Assistance (OFA) runs the Temporary Assistance for Needy Families (TANF) program. Not only does the program provide free job training and education, it helps with locating grants that pay for Child Care. By contacting state agencies, it can find a program that is right for you. You can learn more at: www.acf.hhs.gov/programs/ofa/.

Also, be sure to check out some other opportunities at: www.childcareaware.org.

The Child Care and Development Block Grant (CCDBG) provides funds to assist with Child Care costs as well. The U.S. Department of Health and Human Services is responsible for heading this terrific organization. Every year, financial burden is eased, as families receive up to thousands of dollars to pay their Child Care costs.

Parents are allowed to choose their own Child Care provider, as long as it's legally operating and it meets all state health and safety requirements. More information can be found at: http://www.csrees.usda.gov/childcareafterschoolprograms.cfm.

General Health Care

Besides the many sources for prescriptions, there are also many co-pay programs that offer financial assistance for some health care costs.

Do a Google search of your particular need or concern. If your child is diagnosed with any illness, ask the doctor for resources. Ask the nurses. Ask other families who have been through it. Ask your co-workers, family, friends and neighbors. Someone usually knows someone who has found a Free Money source to get meds, services, clinical trials or samples of drugs.

To give you an idea of what is out there, we have done a search and found many organizations.

Program:	**American Kidney Fund**
Mission:	With help from AKF, dialysis patients are able to maintain their health insurance coverage. AKF also provides assistance with expenses that insurance will not cover, such as transportation to dialysis, medications, special diet, kidney donor expenses, and other treatment essentials. AKF's specialty programs help patients afford treatment during emergency travel and recover from natural disasters.
URL:	www.kidneyfund.org
Email:	patientservice@kidneyfund.org
Address:	6110 Executive Blvd., Suite 1010, Rockville, MD 20852
Phone:	1-800-638-8299
Assistance:	National
	Medicare Prescription Drug Assistance
	Insurance Premium Assistance
	Other Patient Support

Program:	**Association of Community Cancer Centers**
Mission:	ACCC is the national multidisciplinary organization that focuses on enhancing, promoting, and protecting the entire continuum of quality cancer care for patients.
URL:	www.accc-cancer.org
Address:	11600 Nebel Street, Suite 21, Rockville, Maryland, 20852-2557
Phone:	301-984-9496
Fax:	301-770-1949
Assistance:	National
	Prescription Assistance

Program:	**CancerCare**
Mission:	CancerCare is a national nonprofit organization that provides free, professional support services to anyone affected by cancer: people with cancer, caregivers, children, loved ones, and the bereaved. CancerCare programs, including counseling, education, financial assistance, and practical help, are provided by trained oncology social workers and are completely free of charge.
URL:	www.cancercare.org
Email:	info@cancercare.org
Address:	275 Seventh Ave., Floor 22, New York, NY 10001
Phone:	800-813-4673
Fax:	212-712-8495
Assistance:	National
	Prescription Assistance
	Other Patient Support

Program:	**American Childhood Cancer Organization**
Mission:	Our mission is to provide information and awareness for children and adolescents with cancer and their families, to advocate for their needs, and to support research so every child survives and leads a long and healthy life.
URL:	www.acco.org/
Email:	staff@acco.org
Address:	P.O. Box 498, Kensington, MD 20895-0498
Phone:	855-858-2226 or 301-962-3520

Program:	**Caring Voice Coalition, Inc.**
Mission:	Comprehensive help for the needs of patients with serious, chronic illnesses.
URL:	www.caringvoice.org
Email:	CVCInfo@caringvoice.org
Address:	Caring Voice Coalition, Inc., 8249 Meadowbridge Road, Mechanicsville, VA 23116

Phone: (888) 267-1440

Assistance: National
Medicare Prescription Drug Assistance
Insurance Copayment Assistance
Insurance Premium Assistance
Insurance Counseling and Advocacy
Other Patient Support

Program: **Chai Lifeline**

Mission: Chai Lifeline is a not for profit organization dedicated to helping children suffering from serious illness as well as their family members. They offer a comprehensive range of services to address the multiple needs of patients, parents, and siblings.

URL: www.chailifeline.org

Email: info@chailifeline.org

Address: International Office, 151 West 30th Street, New York, NY 10001

Phone: (877) CHAI LIFE

Fax: 212.465.0949

Assistance: National
Insurance Copayment Assistance
Insurance Premium Assistance
Other Patient Support

Program: **Chemocare.com**

Mission: This organization provides links to other resources for prescription assistance.

URL: www.chemocare.com

Program: **Chronic Disease Fund, Inc. (CDF)**

Mission: CDF's focus is to provide assistance to those underinsured patients who are diagnosed with chronic or life altering diseases that require the use of expensive, specialty therapeutics.

URL:	www.cdfund.org
Email:	info@cdfund.org
Address:	10880 John W. Elliott Drive, Suite 400, Frisco, TX 75034
Phone:	877-YOUR-CDF
Assistance:	National
	Prescription Assistance

Program:	**Geriatric Services of America**
Mission:	Help chronic respiratory disease patients by providing education, support, equipment, and life-saving medications quickly and directly to the patient's home.
Address:	Geriatric Services of America, Inc., 5030 S. Mill Ave. D-23, Tempe, AZ 85282
Phone:	1-800-279-1519

Program:	**HealthWell Foundation**
Mission:	The HealthWell Foundation addresses the needs of individuals who cannot afford their insurance copayments, premiums, coinsurance, or other out-of-pocket health care costs.
URL:	www.healthwellfoundation.org
Email:	info@healthwellfoundation.org
Address:	P.O. Box 4133, Gaithersburg, MD 20878
Phone:	1-800-675-8416
Fax:	1-800-282-7692
Assistance:	National
	Insurance Copayment Assistance
	Insurance Premium Assistance
	Prescription Assistance
	Other Patient Support

Program: **Hunterdon County Medication Access Partnership (HCMAP)**

Mission: HCMAP connects concerned individuals, congregations, businesses, and government organizations to increase awareness and access to affordable prescription medication for Hunterdon County residents in need.

Email: mark.peters@bms.com

Address: 23 Timberwick Drive, Flemington, NJ 08822

Phone: 609-897-2866

Assistance: Prescription Assistance

Program: **International Oncology Network (ION)**

Mission: To keep affordable medications within patients' reach, many of ION's pharmaceutical partners offer Patient Assistance Programs to provide free or discounted medications to people who may not be able to afford their needed medications.

URL: www.iononline.com

Email: memberid@iononline.com

Address: International Oncology Network (ION), An AmerisourceBergen Specialty Group Company, 3101 Gaylord Parkway, Frisco, TX 75034

Phone: 888-536-7697 Ext: 6847

Fax: 888-329-3893

Assistance: National
Prescription Assistance

Program: **Leukemia and Lymphoma Society**

Mission: The Leukemia & Lymphoma Society is the world's largest voluntary health organization dedicated to funding blood cancer research, education and patient services. The Society's mission: Cure leukemia, lymphoma, Hodgkin's disease and myeloma, and improve the quality of life of patients and their families. Since its founding in 1949, the Society has invested more than $550.8 million for research specifically targeting blood cancers.

URL:	www.lls.org
Phone:	800-955-4572
Assistance:	National
	Insurance Copayment Assistance
	Insurance Premium Assistance
	Lists Organizations that Provide Insurance,
	Counseling and Advocacy
	Lists Organizations that Provide Prescription Assistance

Program:	**National Children's Cancer Society**
Mission:	The mission of The National Children's Cancer Society is to improve the quality of life for children with cancer and their families by providing financial and in-kind assistance, advocacy, support services, and education.
URL:	www.beyondthecure.org
Email:	survivorship@children-cancer.org
Address:	One South Memorial Drive, Suite 800, St. Louis, MO 63102
Phone:	(800) 5-FAMILY
Fax:	314-241-1996

Program:	**National Organization for Rare Disorders**
Mission:	Mission: The National Organization for Rare Disorders (NORD), a 501(c)3 organization, is a unique federation of voluntary health organizations dedicated to helping people with rare "orphan" diseases and assisting the organizations that serve them. NORD is committed to the identification, treatment, and cure of rare disorders through programs of education, advocacy, research, and service.
URL:	www.rarediseases.org
Address:	55 Kenosia Avenue, P.O. Box 1968, Danbury, CT 06813-1968
Phone:	203-744-0100
Fax:	203-798-2291

Assistance: National
Insurance Copayment Assistance
Insurance Premium Assistance
Prescription Assistance

Program: **NeedyMeds**

Mission: NeedyMeds is a 501(3)(c) non-profit with the mission of helping people who cannot afford medicine or health care costs. The information at NeedyMeds is available anonymously and free of charge.

URL: www.needymeds.org

Email: info@needymeds.org

Address: NeedyMeds, Inc, P.O. Box 219, Gloucester, MA 01931

Phone: 978-865-4115

Fax: 419-858-7221

Assistance: National
Medicare Prescription Drug Assistance
Insurance Copayment Prescription Assistance

Program: **Patient Access Network Foundation (PAN)**

Mission: The Patient Access Network Foundation provides financial support for out-of-pocket costs associated with a wide range of drugs, to treat a number of conditions.

URL: www.panfoundation.org

Email: contact@panfoundation.org

Address: P.O. Box 221858, Charlotte, NC 28222-1858

Phone: 866-316-PANF (7263)

Assistance: National
Prescription Assistance

Program: **Patient Advocate Foundation Co-Pay Relief**

Mission: Patient Advocate Foundation's Co-Pay Relief (CPR) Program provides direct co-payment assistance for pharmaceutical products to insured Americans who financially and medically qualify.

URL:	www.patientadvocate.org
Email:	help@patientadvocate.org
Address:	700 Thimble Shoals Blvd., Suite 200, Newport News, VA 23606
Phone:	800-532-5274
Fax:	757-873-8999
Assistance:	National
	Medicare Prescription Drug Assistance
	Prescription Assistance

Program:	**Patient Services Incorporated**
Mission:	Patient Services Incorporated (PSI) is a non-profit organization primarily dedicated to providing health insurance premium assistance, pharmacy co-payment assistance and co-payment waiver assistance for persons with specific expensive chronic illnesses.
URL:	www.patientservicesinc.org
Email:	uneedpsi@uneedpsi.org
Address:	P.O. Box 1602, Midlothian, VA 23113
Phone:	800-366-7741
Fax:	804-744-5407
Assistance:	National
	Medicare Prescription Drug Assistance
	Insurance Copayment Assistance
	Insurance Premium Assistance
	Insurance Counseling and Advocacy
	Prescription Assistance

Program:	**The Center for Medicare Advocacy**
Mission:	The Center for Medicare Advocacy, Inc. is a national non-profit, non-partisan organization that provides education, advocacy, and legal assistance to help elders and people with disabilities obtain Medicare and necessary health care. The Center was established in 1986.

They focus on the needs of Medicare beneficiaries, people with chronic conditions, and those in need of long-term care. The organization is involved in writing, education, and advocacy activities of importance to Medicare beneficiaries nation-wide. The Center's central office is in Connecticut, with offices in Washington, D.C., and throughout the country.

URL: www.medicareadvocacy.org
Address: P.O. Box 350, Willimantic, CT 06226
Phone: 860-456-7790
Assistance: Medicare Prescription Drug Assistance

As always, contact information changes, but this information was accurate to our knowledge when we went to print. For the most updated list of co-payment programs, visit: http://www.pparx. org/en/prescription_assistance_programs/co-payment_programs

Private Foundations for Medical Help

There are also private foundations that help with medical bills. For example, the Ray Tye Medical Aid Foundation states its mission as: "to facilitate access to medical treatments for financially vulnerable individuals in our society, thereby assuring equal access to specialized, life-saving medical evaluation, diagnosis, treatment and rehabilitation to all."

Everybody deserves decent health care. Everybody, no matter how much (or little) money you have. To request aid, click: http://rtmaf.org/medical-aid-request/.

> Everybody deserves decent health care.

This foundation offers health assistance and hope around the world. In February 2009, a sixteen-year-old girl from Afghanistan was given a new life. She had broken her jaw at age eight, and it had welded together as it healed. She thus had a difficult time eating or speaking, and she was in constant pain.

Thanks to a group called Healing the Children, she was brought to New York for the miracle surgery. The Ray Tye Foundation paid for the surgery, giving her back a normal life. This medical aid foundation and others like it provide medical care for people here and all over the world.

Negotiate Free Services

I always tell people, in any situation, to ask for what they want. If you want help with medical bills, ask!

Let me tell you a true story about a doctor who became the patient with no insurance. It happened. This doc, a plastic surgeon, was switching insurance companies and there was a window of time in between when he had no insurance coverage.

As Murphy's Law would have it, he got hurt. He was playing baseball with his son and somehow fell on his elbow and hurt it badly. He was told he needed surgery immediately. And then he had to confess that he had no insurance.

> If you are up front and frank and willing to negotiate, you may be surprised at the outcome.

It is odd for a doctor to not have insurance. The point here, though, is he didn't just hang his head and pay the huge bills. He did what we all can do. He negotiated his costs!

It didn't matter that he was a doctor. He, as a patient, needed services just like everybody else. He did not want to pay the full cost of the surgery. He talked to the doctors at the immediate care clinic. He got his payment down from $4,800 to $2,400!

When you don't have insurance, there is no middleman. Talk to the doctor and the clinic. Explain that you can pay a discounted amount. There is no insurance company to hassle with, so odds are in your favor. If you are up front and frank and willing to negotiate, you may be surprised at the outcome.

This good doctor said it best: "You should always ask. Why wouldn't you try?"

I agree 100%.

There are places that help you find free care.

- ✔ Patient Advocate Foundation: www.copays.org
- ✔ Patient Services Incorporated: www.patientservicesinc.org

Insurance

When it comes to insurance coverage, you don't have to go without it just because you are in between jobs. You can still have your employer's insurance; the kicker is that, if you go on COBRA insurance, you pay the premium instead of it being paid by your old company.

Many times, it's cheaper to get insurance yourself. Check out this web site to help you get the best deal: ehealthinsurance.com.

There is a lot of great info there!

Maybe you're fit as a fiddle and roll the dice and live without health insurance. You don't want to take that chance with your kids, though. There is a program called SCHIP, State Children's Health Insurance Program, which offers discounted coverage.

The SCHIP web site gives a state-by-state directory of programs. You can check it out at www.insurekidsnow.gov/state or call 877-KIDS-NOW.

There are other government programs, too. Your entire family may qualify for insurance from a state high-risk pool (if you live in a state that has one). To find out about your state, check out www.naschip.org/states_pools.htm.

If you have a specific disease, there are foundations that provide financial aid for your medical treatment. Some of those organizations include:

- ✔ Heart Disease: Heart Support of America (http://heartsupportofamerica.org)

- ✔ Kidney Disease: American Kidney Fund (www.kidneyfund.org)

- ✔ HIV/AIDS: The Access Project (www.accessproject.org)

- ✔ Hepatitis: The Access Project (www.accessproject.org)

- ✔ Cancer: Cancer Care Assist (www.cancercare.org/financial)

- ✔ Various Diseases: Caring Voice Coalition (www.caringvoice.org)

- ✔ Other rare diseases: National Organization for Rare Diseases (http://rarediseases.org)

- ✔ Vision Care: EyeCare America and Vision USA (www.eyecareamerica.org)

Government Funded Health Care

There are federally funded health care centers all across the US. Even if you have no medical insurance, you pay what you can afford, based on your income. These health centers are located in cities and rural areas. They provide regular checkups, treatment when you are sick, full pregnancy care and well-baby checkups and immunizations for your children. There is also dental care, mental health and substance abuse treatment and prescription drugs... so pretty much the whole gamut of care.

> These health centers are located in cities and rural areas.

To find a free clinic near you, type in your address at Find a Health Center: http://findahealthcenter.hrsa.gov/Search_HCC.aspx

Many people are out of work these days and that means people are going without insurance. It doesn't have to be so. Did you know that many part-time employers give benefits? You can get health insurance, even if you don't work full time. Here is a sample of who pays part-timers benefits: Target, Starbucks, Lowe's, IKEA, Trader Joe's, Whole Foods, Barnes & Noble, Nordstrom, Land's End, Nike and JCPenney.

Dental

Another aspect of health care is dental expenses. Going to the dentist can be expensive, so some people put it off and then a small problem becomes a major toothache!

Taking a peek at www.medicare.gov, you will learn that there are programs that help out millions of folks. State Medicaid programs assist with medical and dental expenses and eyeglasses.

The National Foundation of Dentistry for the Handicapped (NFDH) provides services to the elderly, the disabled and others. There is a network of thousands of dentists who donate their time and even make house calls. For more information on this network and their service, visit www.nfdh.org. You can link directly to your state to find donated services in your community.

Dental schools are another great source of free services or highly discounted dental care. If you have a dental college in your community or a neighboring one, it could be worth your while to check it out and make the drive. Dental expenses, if paid in full, can be outrageous. Why pay full price, if you don't have to? To find a dental college near you, visit: www.adea.org.

We just did a quick Google search and found a blogger who had listed a comprehensive list of free and low-fee dental care sites. Thank you, blogger! The information was good at the time so, if a number has gone out of service, do another online search for that particular provider for more current information. The idea is that help is out there.

Assistance programs vary from state to state. Call your state Dental Society for programs in your area.

- ✔ Alabama Dental Association: 334-265-1684

- ✔ Alaska Dental Society: 800-478-4675

- ✔ Arizona State Dental Association: 602-957-4777

- ✔ Arkansas State Dental Association: 501-771-7650

- ✔ California Dental Association: 800-736-8702

- ✔ California Society of Pediatric Dentist: 310-548-0134

- ✔ Fresno Madera Dental Association: 209-438-7284

- ✔ Humbolt-Del Norte Dental Society: 707-443-7476

- ✔ Orange County Dental Society: 714-634-8944

- ✔ Tri-County Dental Society: 909-370-2112 (serving Riverside, San Bernardino and the Eastern Portion of Los Angeles County)

✔ Colorado Dental Association: 303-740-6900

✔ Connecticut Dental Association: 203-278-5550

✔ Delaware State Dental Society: 302-654-4335

✔ District of Columbia Dental Society: 202-547-7613

✔ Florida Dental Association: 800- 877-9922

✔ Georgia Dental Association: 404-636-7553

✔ Hawaii Dental Association: 808-536-2135; 800-359-6725

✔ Idaho State Dental Association: 208-343-7543

✔ Illinois State Dental Society: 217-525-1406; 800-475-4737

✔ Indiana Dental Association; 317-634-2610; 800-562-5646

✔ Iowa Dental Association: 515-282-7250; 800-828-2181

✔ Kansas Dental Association: 913-272-7360

✔ Kentucky Dental Association: 502-459-5373; 800-292-1855

✔ Louisiana Dental Association: 504-926-1986; 800-388-6642

✔ Maine Dental Association: 207-622-7900; 800-369-8217

✔ Maryland State Dental Association: 410-964-2880; 800-766-2880

✔ Massachusetts Dental Society: 508-651-7511; 800-342- 8747

✔ Southeastern District of the Massachusetts Dental Society: 508-674-8818

✔ Michigan Dental Association: 517-372-9070; 800-589-2632

✔ Minnesota Dental Association: 612-646-7454; 800-950-3368

✔ Mississippi Dental Association: 1-601-982-0442

✔ Missouri Dental Association: 314-634-3436; 800-688-1907

✔ Montana Dental Association: 406-443-2061

✔ Nebraska Dental Association: 402-476-1704

✔ Nevada Dental Association: 702-255-4211; 800-962-6710

✔ New Hampshire Dental Society: 603-255-4211; 800-244-5961

✔ New Jersey Dental Association: 908-821-9400

✔ New Mexico Dental Association: 505-294-1368

✔ New York State Academy of General Dentistry: 518-465-0044; 800-255-2100

✔ Suffolk County Dental Society: 631-232-1400

✔ North Carolina Dental Society: 919-832-1222

✔ North Dakota Dental Association: 701-223-8870

✔ Ohio Dental Association: 614-486-2700

✔ Oklahoma Dental Association: 405-848-8873; 800-876-8890

✔ Oregon Dental Association: 503-620-3230

✔ Pennsylvania Academy of General Dentistry: 215-443-0667

✔ Dental Society of Western Pennsylvania: 412-321-5810

✔ Rhode Island Dental Association: 401-732-6833

✔ South Carolina Dental Association: 803-750-2277; 800-327-2598

✔ South Dakota Dental Association: 605-224-9133

✔ Tennessee Dental Association: 615-383-8962

✔ Texas Dental Association: 512-443-3675; 800-460-8700

✔ Greater Houston Dental Society: 713-961-4337

✔ Utah Dental Association: 801-261-5315; 800-662-6500

✔ Vermont State Dental Society: 802-864-0115

✔ Virginia Dental Association: 804-358-4927

✔ Washington State Dental Association: 206-448-1914; 800-448-3368

✔ West Virginia Dental Association: 304-344-5246

✔ Wisconsin Dental Association: 414-276-4520; 800-364-7646

✔ Wyoming Dental Association: 307-634-5878; 800-244-0779

Following is a listing of donated dental services in your state:

✔ Alabama: 334-834-1114

✔ Alaska: 907-561-6028

✔ Arkansas: 501-221-0280

✔ California: 888-471-6334

✔ Colorado-Denver area: 303-534-5297; Outside Denver: 303-534-3863

✔ Florida: 305-598-7080

✔ Hawaii: 888-471-6334

✔ Illinois-Chicago area: 800-893-1685; rest of the state: 309-689-6785

✔ Indiana: 317-631-6022

✔ Kansas: 785-273-1900

✔ Louisiana: 504-948-6141

✔ Maine: 207-620-8276

✔ Maryland: 410-964-1944

✔ Michigan-Detroit area: 248-489-2204; Outside Detroit: 248-489-2206

✔ Mississippi: 601-368-9823

✔ Nevada: 702-651-5744

✔ Montana: 406-449-9670

✔ New Hampshire: 603-223-1531

✔ New Jersey: 732-940-0055; or 732-821-2977

✔ New Mexico: 505-298-7206

✔ North Dakota: 888-471-6334

✔ Ohio: 513-621-2517

✔ Oregon: 503-774-3898

✔ Pennsylvania-Western Penn: 412-243-4866; Eastern Penn: 717-238-8721

✔ Rhode Island: 401-728-9448

✔ South Dakota: 605-357-8660

✔ Texas: 512-912-1358

✔ Virginia: 804-264-9010

✔ Washington: 206 441-8777

✔ West Virginia: 304-296-9005

✔ Wisconsin-Milwaukee area: 414-276-0370; rest of the state: 262-670-0837

✔ Wyoming: 307-766-2829

Eyeglasses

Sometimes people put off eye exams and new glasses because of the expense, too. Pearle Vision and LensCrafters both offer discounts to seniors and other groups. If you are a senior, you get LOTS of Free Money discounts through AARP, the Association of American Retired Persons. Take advantage. Go to www.aarp.org/.

AAA members get discounts on eyeglasses through these locations. They apply to kids, too! Check out your AAA membership or look it up online. You can also go online to Pearle Vision or LensCrafters (www.pearlevision.com and www.lenscrafters.com) or go to the store location in your town.

If you have a Sear's store with an eyeglass store, they offer discounts, too, through AAA! (www.searsoptical.com)

Pay attention to your local stores and community organizations. Different opportunities are available at different times of the year. Just ask… in person, online or over the phone. Talk to friends, coworkers and family. They can be great sources for freebies.

If you or your child is in need of eyeglasses, check with your state for assistance. Many states have programs that provide free eye exams and/or glasses. Check with your county as well. Maybe your health care clinic has a program or can steer you to one.

> Many states have programs that provide free eye exams and/or glasses.

Don't forget that most local Lion's Clubs (www.lionsclubs.org) provide free eyeglasses to their local communities. If you need an exam, try Vision USA. You apply and after they process your request, you receive a form that you take to a local eye doctor for a free eye exam for you or your child.

A volunteer organization called Prevent Blindness works with state, local and national governments to provide eye screenings and eye care. They have several networks within local communities. For further details, visit:

- ✔ www.preventblindness.org
- ✔ www.diabetes-sight.org
- ✔ The PBA Vision Health Resource Center (1-800-331-2020)

As you can see (pun intended), there are many places out there willing and waiting to assist you with glasses and/or eye exams. There is another organization that claims, "We help when no one else can." For eyeglasses and eye exams, you can contact New Eyes for the Needy. To apply, you can contact a social service agency in your area, the school's nurse at your child's school or contact the organization directly at www.neweyesfortheneedy.org. You can also send in your application form and prescription to:

New Eyes for the Needy
549 Millburn Avenue
P.O. Box 332
Short Hills, NJ 07078

I hope this makes you realize that there are many ways to get what you want and that you don't have to pay an arm and a leg for it. Use your creativity when thinking up resources, and always ask that resource to refer you to the next one.

Legal Services

Sometimes in life, there comes a need for legal advice. However, lawyers, as we all know, can be very expensive. You don't want to pay some guy by the minute when there are free options available to you.

The American Bar Association has a network of legal professionals who do pro bono work (that means you do not pay). You can search state by state to find legal help in your community. Visit the following site and click on your state:

http://apps.americanbar.org/legalservices/probono/directory. html.

Another option is http://apps.americanbar.org/legalservices/findlegalhelp/home.cfm. This site, too, has links to free legal help in your state.

All states have free legal services. An amazing amount of legal aid is offered in almost every community. Go online or ask around for resources and referrals. It's mind blowing what you can find with an Internet search. No matter where you live, you can click and pick from a wealth of agencies.

For example, if you live in California, with one click and in a matter of seconds, you can look into all of the following:

Greater Bakersfield Legal Assistance Inc.
615 California Avenue Bakersfield, CA 93304
805-325-5943
www.gbla.org

Central California Legal Services
1401 Fulton Street, Suite 700
Fresno, CA 93721
559-441-1611
www.centralcallegal.org

Neighborhood Legal Services of Los Angeles County
1102 E. Chevy Chase Drive
Glendale, CA 91205
818-896-5211
www.nls-la.org

Inland Counties Legal Services, Inc.
1040 Iowa Avenue, Suite 109
Riverside, CA 92507
909-368-2555
www.inlandlegal.org

Legal Services of Northern California, Inc.
517 12th Street Sacramento, CA 95814
916-551-2150
www.lsnc.net

Legal Aid Society of Orange County, Inc.
2101 N. Tustin Ave.
Santa Ana, CA 92705
800-834-5001
www.legal-aid.com

California Indian Legal Services, Inc.
609 S. Escondido Blvd.
Escondido, CA 92025
760-746-8941
www.calindian.org

Bay Area Legal Aid
405 14th Street, 9th Floor
Oakland, CA
510-663-4744
www.baylegal.org

Legal Aid Foundation of Los Angeles
1102 South Crenshaw Boulevard
Los Angeles, CA 90019-3111
800-399-4529
www.lafla.org

Legal Aid Society of San Diego, Inc.
110 South Euclid Avenue
San Diego, CA 92114
619-262-0896
www.lassd.org

California Rural Legal Assistance, Inc.
631 Howard Street, Suite 300
San Francisco, CA 94105-3907
415-777-2752
www.crla.org

Also, for free legal aid referrals and information in California, you can visit http://lawhelpca.org/. See what I mean by how much information is available? That is just for one state.

Another search method is to Google "legal aid" followed by the name of your county in your state.

Just to show the wealth of information and legal service opportunities, I clicked on Pro Bono for California again from the same site, http://apps.americanbar.org/legalservices/findlegalhelp/home.cfm. Here are the results (source: http://apps.americanbar.org/legalservices/findlegalhelp/pb.cfm?id=CA):

Statewide

California Lawyers for the Arts
Primary Address: Fort Mason Center,
Building C, Room 265 [State Headquarters]
City: San Francisco
State: CA
Zip code: 94123
General Phone: 415-775-7200
Fax: 415-775-1143
Intake Phone: 415-775-7200 x107
Counties Served: Statewide
Case Types: Art law, Entertainment law,
Intellectual Property law (copyright, trade-
mark, rights of publicity, etc.)
Case Restrictions: C.L.A. only serves
CREATIVE ARTISTS and ARTS
ORGANIZATIONS as well as general indi-
viduals with arts related issues.
Web Site: http://www.calawyersforthearts.org/

California Lawyers for the Arts
Primary Address: 1641 18th St
City: Santa Monica
State: CA
Zip code: 90404-3807
General Phone: 310-998-5590
Fax: 310-998-5594
Intake Phone: 310-998-5590
Counties Served: Statewide
Case Types: Art law, Entertainment law,
Intellectual Property law (copyright, trade
mark, rights of publicity, etc.)
Case Restrictions: C.L.A. only serves
CREATIVE ARTISTS and ARTS
ORGANIZATIONS as well as general indi-
viduals with arts related issues.
Web Site: http://www.calawyersforthearts.org/

Disability Rights Education and Defense
Fund, Inc.
Primary Address: 2212 6th St.
City: Berkeley
State: CA
Zip code: 94710-2219 General Phone:
510-644-2555 Fax: 510-841-8645 Counties
Served: Nationwide
Case Types: Education, Individual Rights
Other Case Types: Civil Rights, Disability
Web Site: http://www.dredf.org

ORAM International (Organization For
Refuge Asylum & Migration)

Primary Address: 39 Drumm Street
City: San Francisco
State: CA
Zip code: 94111
General Phone: (415) 399-1701
Fax: (415) 371-9191
Counties Served: National, International
Other Case Types: Asylum, Immigration
Case Restrictions: ORAM is currently
providing representation and assistance to
lesbians, gays, bisexual, transgender, and
intersex (LGBTI) refugees and asylum seekers.
We serve our clients without regard to race,
religion, nationality, ethnicity, gender, age
or political persuasion. We work to assure
the safety and security of all persons who fall
within our mission.
Web Site: http://www.oraminternational.org
Organization Email: info@oraminternational.
org

San Francisco Lawyers Committee Emergency
Political Asylum Program
Primary Address: 301 Mission St
City: San Francisco
State: CA
Zip code: 94105
General Phone: 415-543-9444
Fax: 415-543-0296
Counties Served: San Francisco
Case Types: Immigration

Alameda

Alameda County Bar Association Volunteer
Legal Services Corporation
Primary Address: 610 Sixteenth Street 426
City: Oakland
State: CA
Zip code: 94612
General Phone: 510-893-7160
Fax: 510-893-3119
Intake Phone: 510-893-7160
Counties Served: Alameda
Case Types: Adoption, Bankruptcy,
Community Economic Development,
Consumer, Child Custody, Dissolution of
Marriage, Domestic Violence, Elder Law,
Housing, Immigration, Public Benefits
Case Restrictions: LSC restrictions. 1) Must
be residents of Alameda County or have a case
in Alameda County. 2) income restrictions =
125% of the federal poverty level.
Web Site: http://www.acbanet.org

Bay Area Legal Aid
Primary Address: 405 14th St., 9th Floor
City: Oakland
State: CA
Zip code: 94612
General Phone: 510-663-4751
Fax: 510-663-4711
Counties Served: Alameda, Contra Costa,
Marin, Napa, San Francisco, San Mateo,
Santa Clara
Case Types: Domestic Violence, Housing,
Public Benefits
Case Restrictions: Low-income
Web Site: http://www.baylegal.org

Bay Area Legal Aid Alameda Regional Office
Primary Address: 405 14th Street, 11th Floor
City: Oakland
State: CA
Zip code: 94612
General Phone: 510-663-4755
Intake Phone: 800-551-5554
Counties Served: Alameda, Contra Costa, San
Francisco, San Mateo, Santa Clara
Case Types: Domestic Violence, Housing,
Public Benefits
Case Restrictions: Low-income
Web Site: http://www.baylegal.org

Bay Area Legal Aid Contra Costa Regional
Office
Primary Address: 1017 MacDonald Avenue
City: Richmond
State: CA
Zip code: 94801
General Phone: 510-233-9954
Counties Served: Contra Costa
Case Types: Domestic Violence, Housing,
Public Benefits
Case Restrictions: Low income
Web Site: http://www.baylegal.org

Bay Area Legal Aid Marin/Napa Regional
Office
Primary Address: 30 North San Pedro Road,
Suite 250
City: San Rafael
State: CA
Zip code: 94903
General Phone: 415-479-8224
Counties Served: Marin
Case Types: Domestic Violence, Housing,
Public Benefits
Case Restrictions: Low-income
Web Site: http://www.baylegal.org

Bay Area Legal Aid Pittsburg Office
Primary Address: 1901 Railroad Avenue,
Suite D
City: Pittsburg
State: CA
Zip code: 94565
General Phone: 925-432-1123
Counties Served: Contra Costa
Case Types: Domestic Violence, Housing,
Public Benefits
Case Restrictions: Low-income
Web Site: http://www.baylegal.org

Bay Area Legal Aid San Francisco Regional
Office
Primary Address: 50 Fell Street, 1st Floor
City: San Francisco
State: CA
Zip code: 94102
General Phone: 415-982-1300
Counties Served: San Francisco
Case Types: Domestic Violence, Housing,
Public Benefits
Case Restrictions: Low-income
Web Site: http://www.baylegal.org

Bay Area Legal Aid San Mateo Regional
Office
Primary Address: 2287 El Camino Real
City: San Mateo
State: CA
Zip code: 94403
General Phone: 650-358-0745
Counties Served: San Mateo
Case Types: Domestic Violence, Housing,
Public Benefits
Case Restrictions: Low-income
Web Site: http://www.baylegal.org

Bay Area Legal Aid Santa Clara Regional
Office
Primary Address: 2 West Santa Clara Street,
8th Floor
City: San Jose
State: CA
Zip code: 95113
General Phone: 408-283-3700
Counties Served: Santa Clara
Case Types: Domestic Violence, Housing,
Public Benefits
Case Restrictions: Low-income
Web Site: http://www.baylegal.org

East Bay Community Law Center
Primary Address: 3130 Shattuck Ave.
City: Berkeley
State: CA
Zip code: 94705-1823
General Phone: 510-548-4040
Fax: 510-548-2566
Intake Phone: 510-548-4040
Counties Served: Alameda
Case Types: AIDS/HIV, Community
Economic Development, Health,
Immigration, Public Benefits, Wills
Case Restrictions: Certain services are
restricted to people living with HIV; oth-
erwise, LSC financial eligibility guidelines
generally apply.
Web Site: http://www.ebclc.org
Organization Email: info@ebclc.org

Family Violence Law Center
Primary Address: PO Box 22009
City: Oakland
State: CA
Zip code: 94623
General Phone: 510-208-0220
Fax: 510-540-5373
Intake Phone: 510-540-5370
Counties Served: Alameda
Case Types: Child Custody, Dissolution of
Marriage, Domestic Violence, Elder Law,
Housing, Immigration, Public Benefits,
Termination of Parental Rights
Case Restrictions: Clients must have domestic
violence case/issue to receive other legal/social
services.

Legal Assistance for Seniors
Primary Address: 464 7th Street
City: Oakland
State: CA
Zip code: 94607
General Phone: 510-832-3040
Fax: 510-987-7399
Intake Phone: 510-832-3040
Counties Served: Alameda
Case Types: Elder Abuse, Guardianships,
Health, Immigration, Public Benefits
Case Restrictions: Age 60 or over (no age
restriction for Guardianships)
Website: http://www.lashicap.org

Contra Costa
BWA-Legal Advocacy Program
Primary Address: PO Box 6556

City: Concord
State: CA
Zip code: 94524-1556
General Phone: 925-676-3122
Fax: 925-676-0564
Intake Phone: 925-676-3122
Counties Served: Contra Costa
Case Types: Child Custody, Dissolution of
Marriage, Domestic Violence
Case Restrictions: Family law issues

Contra Costa Senior Legal Services
Primary Address: 4006 MacDonald Ave.
City: Richmond
State: CA
Zip code: 94805
General Phone: 510-374-3712
Fax: 510-374-3304
Intake Phone: 510-374-3712
Counties Served: Contra Costa
Case Types: Consumer, Elder Law, Housing,
Individual Rights, Public Benefits, Wills
Other Case Types: Elder Abuse
Case Restrictions: Client must be 60 and
resident of Contra Costa County.
Web Site: http://www.seniorlegalservices.org

Fresno
Central California Legal Services Inc. —
Voluntary Legal Services Program
Primary Address: 1999 Tuolumne Street 700
City: Fresno
State: CA
Zip code: 93721
General Phone: 559-570-1200
Fax: 559-570-1254
Intake Phone: 559-570-1200
Counties Served: Fresno, Kings, Mariposa,
Merced, Tulare, Tuolumne
Case Types: Bankruptcy, Community
Economic Development, Consumer, Child
Custody, Domestic Violence, Education,
Elder Law, Employment, Health, Housing,
Immigration, Public Benefits, Real Estate,
Wills
Other Case Types: Conservatorships,
Guardianships, Domestic Violence
Restraining Orders
Case Restrictions: Financial eligibility &
citizenship/LPR.
Web Site: http://www.centralcallegal.org
Organization Email: fresno@centralcallegal.org

Humboldt

Humboldt County Bar Association
Primary Address: PO Box 1017
City: Eureka
State: CA
Zip code: 95502-1017
General Phone: 707-445-2652
Fax: 707-445-0935
Counties Served: Humboldt Case Types:
Consumer, Health, Housing, Real Estate,
Torts, Wills

North Coast AIDS Project
Primary Address: 529 I St.
City: Eureka
State: CA
Zip code: 95501
General Phone: 707-268-2132
Fax: 707-445-6097
Intake Phone: 707-268-2132
Counties Served: Del Norte, Humboldt
Case Types: AIDS/HIV
Other Case Types: File for do not resuscitate,
etc., power of attorney, worker's comp.
Case Restrictions: Must be HIV+

Los Angeles

Asian Pacific American Legal Center of
Southern California
Primary Address: 1145 Wilshire Blvd., 2nd
Floor
City: Los Angeles
State: CA
Zip code: 90015
General Phone: 213-977-7500
Fax: 213-977-7595
Case Types: Consumer, Child Custody,
Dissolution of Marriage, Domestic Violence,
Employment, Health, Housing, Immigration,
Public Benefits
Case Restrictions: Language capability, no
class action for civil rights cases, conflict of
interest.
Web Site: http://www.advancedjustice-la.org

Bet Tzedek Legal Services
Primary Address: 3250 Wilshire Blvd., 13th
Floor
City: Los Angeles
State: CA
Zip code: 90010-1509
General Phone: 323-939-0506
Fax: 323-939-1040

Counties Served: Los Angeles
Case Types: AIDS/HIV, Adoption,
Bankruptcy, Consumer, Elder Law,
Employment, Housing, Public Benefits, Real
Estate, Wills
Other Case Types: Employment rights,
Caregiver issues
Case Restrictions: Clients must be residents
of LA County, all must be prescreened prior
to being given appointment, case must have
merit.
Web Site: http://www.bettzedek.org

Break The Cycle
Primary Address: P.O. Box 64996
City: Los Angeles
State: CA
Zip code: 90064
General Phone: 310-286-3366
Fax: 310-286-3386
Intake Phone: 1-888-988-8336
Counties Served: Los Angeles
Case Types: Domestic Violence
Other Case Types: Domestic Violence related
cases for Youth Ages 12-22
Case Restrictions: Client must live with the
Los Angeles County and must be within the
ages of 12-22 and have experienced Domestic
Violence.
Web Site: http://www.breakthecycle.org

Burbank Bar Association Lawyer Referral
Service and Legal Aid
Primary Address: 2219 W Olive Ave., Suite
100
City: Burbank
State: CA
Zip code: 91506-2625
General Phone: 818-843-0931
Fax: 818/843-5852
Counties Served: Los Angeles

City of Santa Fe Springs Legal Services
Program
Primary Address: 9255 Pioneer Blvd.
City: Santa Fe Springs
State: CA
Zip code: 90670-2380
General Phone: 562-692-0261
Fax: 562-695-8620
Case Restrictions: Must live in Santa Fe
Springs and program services unincorporated
areas of Whittier, the town of Los Neitos, and
the city of Pico Rivera.

Organization Email: familyandhumanservices@santafesprings.org

Community Legal Services
Primary Address: 11834 Firestone Blvd.
City: Norwalk
State: CA
Zip code: 90650-2901
General Phone: 562-864-9935
Fax: 562/863-8853
Intake Phone: 800-834-5001
Counties Served: Los Angeles
Case Types: Consumer, Child Custody,
Dissolution of Marriage, Domestic Violence,
Health, Housing, Individual Rights, Public
Benefits
Case Restrictions: We are not able to serve
undocumented individuals.

Disability Rights Legal Center
Primary Address: 919 S Albany St
City: Los Angeles
State: CA
Zip code: 90015
General Phone: 213-736-1031 (V & TDD)
Fax: 213-736-1428
Intake Phone: 213-736-1334
Counties Served: Kern, Los Angeles, Orange,
San Bernadino, San Diego, Ventura
Case Types: Housing, Individual Rights
Other Case Types: Cancer Advocacy,
Disability Rights, Special Education
Web Site: http://www.disabilityrightslegal-
center.org

El Rescate Legal Services
Primary Address: 1340 S Bonnie Brae St.
City: Los Angeles
State: CA
Zip code: 90006-5403
General Phone: 213-387-3284
Fax: 213-387-9189
Counties Served: Los Angeles
Case Types: Immigration
Case Restrictions: We do not accept cases of
those who persecuted others.
Harriett Buhai Center for Family Law
Primary Address: 3250 Wilshire Blvd., Suite
710
City: Los Angeles
State: CA
Zip code: 90010
General Phone: 213 388-7505
Fax: 323-939-2199

Intake Phone: 213 388-7515
Counties Served: Los Angeles
Case Types: Child Custody, Dissolution of
Marriage, Domestic Violence
Web Site: http://www.hbcfl.org

HIV & AIDS Legal Services Alliance, Inc.
(HALSA)
Primary Address: 3550 Wilshire Blvd. 750
City: Los Angeles
State: CA
Zip code: 90010
General Phone: 213-201-1640
Fax: 213-993-1594
Intake Phone: 213-201-1640
Counties Served: Los Angeles
Case Types: AIDS/HIV, Employment, Health,
Housing, Immigration, Individual Rights,
Public Benefits, Wills
Other Case Types: Tax form preparation
Case Restrictions: Must be HIV+, low-income
and live in Los Angeles County.
Web Site: http://www.halsaservices.org

Immigration Legal Assistance Project
Primary Address: 300 N Los Angeles St., Suite
3107
City: Los Angeles
State: CA
Zip code: 90012-3335
General Phone: 213-485-1872
Fax: 213-485-0047
Intake Phone: 213-485-1872
Counties Served: Los Angeles
Case Types: AIDS/HIV, Immigration
Web Site: http://www.lacba.org

Inner City Law Center
Primary Address: 1325 E 7th St.
City: Los Angeles
State: CA
Zip code: 90021-1101
General Phone: 213-891-2880
Fax: 213-891-2888
Intake Phone: 213-891-2880
Counties Served: Los Angeles
Case Types: Housing, Public Benefits

Legal Aid Foundation of Los Angeles
Primary Address: 1102 Crenshaw Blvd.
City: Los Angeles
State: CA
Zip code: 90019-3111
General Phone: 323-801-7924

Fax: 323-801-7945
Intake Phone: 800-399-4529
Counties Served: Los Angeles
Case Types: Community Economic
Development, Consumer, Child Custody,
Dissolution of Marriage, Domestic Violence,
Employment, Health, Housing, Immigration,
Individual Rights, Public Benefits, Real Estate,
Termination of Parental Rights, Torts
Case Restrictions: Cannot serve undocu-
mented aliens.

Legal Services Program for Pasadena and San
Gabriel-Pomona Valley
Primary Address: 243 W Mission Blvd., Suite
303
City: Pomona
State: CA
Zip code: 91766-1560
General Phone: 909-622-7455
Fax: 909-469-1729
Intake Phone: 909-622-1417
Counties Served: Los Angeles
Case Types: Bankruptcy, Child Custody,
Dissolution of Marriage, Domestic
Violence Other Case Types: Post-decree
modifications of custody/visitation
Case Restrictions: Must reside in service area;
jurisdiction over case must be either close to a
volunteer attorney or accepted for representa-
tion by a Legal Aid/Legal Service program in a
foreign jurisdiction.

Los Angeles Center for Law and Justice
Primary Address: 2606 E 1st St.
City: Los Angeles
State: CA
Zip code: 90033-3506
General Phone: 213-266-2690
Fax: 213-266-2695
Counties Served: Los Angeles
Case Types: Consumer, Dissolution of
Marriage, Domestic Violence, Housing,
Public Benefits, Real Estate
Case Restrictions: Must live in service areas:
90031, 90032, 90033, 90041, 90042, 90063,
90065, 90023, 90039 (Atwater only)

Los Angeles County Bar Association Barristers
AIDS Legal Services Project
Primary Address: PO Box 55020
City: Los Angeles
State: CA
Zip code: 90055-2020

General Phone: 213-896-6436
Fax: 213-896-6500
Counties Served: Los Angeles
Case Types: AIDS/HIV

Los Angeles County Bar Association Barristers
Domestic Violence Project
Primary Address: 261 S Figueroa St.
City: Los Angeles
State: CA
Zip code: 90014-1648
General Phone: 213-896-6491
Fax: 213-896-6500
Intake Phone: 213-624-3665
Counties Served: Los Angeles
Case Types: Domestic Violence
Web Site: http://lacba.org

Los Angeles Gay and Lesbian Center Legal
Services Department
Primary Address: 1625 Schrader Blvd.
City: Los Angeles
State: CA
Zip code: 90028-6213
General Phone: 213-993-7670
Fax: 213-933-7699
Counties Served: Los Angeles
Case Types: Child Custody, Dissolution of
Marriage, Domestic Violence, Housing,
Immigration, Individual Rights, Wills

Neighborhood Legal Services of Los Angeles
County
Primary Address: 13327 Van Nuys Blvd.
City: Pacoima
State: CA
Zip code: 91331-3099
General Phone: 818-896-5211
Fax: 818-896-6647
Intake Phone: 800-433-6251
Counties Served: Los Angeles
Case Types: Community Economic
Development, Consumer, Child Custody,
Dissolution of Marriage, Domestic Violence,
Education, Employment, Health, Housing,
Immigration, Individual Rights, Juvenile,
Public Benefits, Termination of Parental Rights
Other Case Types: Discrimination, Family
Law, Community Legal Education
Case Restrictions: NLS is subject to the Legal
Service Corporation (LSC) guidelines on
financial and alien eligibility.
Web Site: http://www.nls-la.org
Organization Email: nls@nls-la.org

Pasadena Human Services Department
Consumer Action Center
Primary Address: 1020 N Fair Oaks Ave.
City: Pasadena
State: CA
Zip code: 91103-3011
General Phone: 626-744-7300
Fax: 626-798-5834
Counties Served: Los Angeles
Case Types: Consumer, Domestic Violence,
Housing, Public Benefits

Police Watch - Police Misconduct Lawyer
Referral Service
Primary Address: 611 S Catalina St.
City: Los Angeles
State: CA
Zip code: 90005-1730
General Phone: 213-387-3435
Fax: 213-387-9085
Intake Phone: 213-387-3325
Counties Served: Kern, Los Angeles, Orange,
Riverside, San Bernardino, San Diego,
Ventura
Case Types: Individual Rights
Other Case Types: Police Misconduct, Civil
Rights Violations.
Case Restrictions: No restrictions: we accept
cases regarding police misconduct. No fees
charged for case acceptance.

Public Counsel Law Center
Primary Address: 601 S Ardmore Ave.
City: Los Angeles
State: CA
Zip code: 90005-2323
General Phone: 213-385-2977
Fax: 213-385-9089
Counties Served: Los Angeles
Case Types: Adoption, Bankruptcy,
Community Economic Development,
Consumer, Domestic Violence, Education,
Elder Law, Health, Housing, Immigration,
Juvenile, Public Benefits, Real Estate,
Termination of Parental Rights, Torts, Wills
Other Case Types: School expulsion,
SIJS, VAWA, Transactional, Contracts,
Expungments, Zoning, Land Use, Tax,
Notario Fraud, Auto Fraud, Guardian Ad
Litem and Guardianship.
Case Restrictions: Financial eligibility (at or
below the federal income guide lines). We do
not take criminal cases.
Web Site: http://www.publiccounsel.org
Organization Email: web@publiccounsel.org

San Fernando Valley Bar Association LRIS
Primary Address: 21300 Oxnard St. Suite 250
City: Woodland Hills
State: CA
Zip code: 91367
General Phone: 818-227-0490
Fax: 818-227-0499
Intake Phone: 818-340-4529
Counties Served: Los Angeles, Ventura
Case Types: AIDS/HIV, Adoption,
Bankruptcy, Community Economic
Development, Consumer, Child Custody,
Domestic Violence, Education, Elder Law,
Employment, Health, Housing, Immigration,
Individual Rights, Juvenile, Public Benefits,
Real Estate, Termination of Parental Rights,
Torts, Wills
Web Site: http://www.sfvba.org/Public%20
Resources/needalawyer.aspx

The Alliance For Children's Rights
Primary Address: 3333 Wilshire Boulevard
550
City: Los Angeles
State: CA
Zip code: 90010 General
Phone: 213-368-6010
Intake Phone: (213) 368-6010
Counties Served: Los Angeles
Case Types: Education, Health, Juvenile
Case Restrictions: Impoverished and abused
children and youths
Web Site: http://kids-alliance.org/

Marin

Legal Aid of Marin County
Primary Address: 30 N San Pedro Rd. 220
City: San Rafael
State: CA
Zip code: 94903
General Phone: 415-492-0230
Fax: 415-492-0947
Intake Phone: 800-498-7666
Counties Served: Marin
Case Types: Bankruptcy, Consumer, Domestic
Violence, Employment, Health, Housing,
Immigration, Individual Rights, Juvenile, Real
Estate, Termination of Parental Rights, Torts,
Wills
Case Restrictions: Financial eligibility, county
residency.
Web Site: http://www.legalaidmarin.org
Organization Email: justice@legal-aid.marin.
ca.us

Mendocino

Legal Services of Northern California
Primary Address: 421 N Oak St.
City: Ukiah
State: CA
Zip code: 95482-4303
General Phone: 707-462-1471
Fax: 707-462-9483
Intake Phone: 877-529-7700
Counties Served: Lake, Mendocino Case
Types: Community Economic Development,
Consumer, Health, Housing, Public Benefits
Case Restrictions: LSC restrictions
Web Site: http://lsnc.net Organization
Organization Email: ukiah-office@lsnc.net

Merced

Central California Legal Services
Primary Address: 357 W Main St. Suite 201
City: Merced
State: CA
Zip code: 95340
General Phone: 209-723-5466
Fax: 559-723-1315
Counties Served: Mariposa, Merced,
Tuolumne
Case Types: Bankruptcy
Other Case Types: Low-income tax problems
Case Restrictions: We are restricted to serving
only those who qualify for services under LSC
guidelines. They must be low income and a
U.S. Citizen or lawful permanent resident.
Web Site: http://www.centralcallegal.org

Mono

Mono County Bar Association Legal Advice
and Referral Clinic
Primary Address: PO Box 3337
City: Mammoth Lakes
State: CA
Zip code: 93546-3337
General Phone: 760-934-4558
Fax: 760-934-2530
Counties Served: Mono
Case Types: Consumer, Dissolution of
Marriage, Domestic Violence, Housing,
Individual Rights

Monterey

Legal Aid of the Central Coast Pro Bono
Program of Monterey County

Primary Address: 2100 Garden Rd., Bldg. B
City: Monterey
State: CA
Zip code: 93940-5366
General Phone: 408-375-0505 (Monterey)
Fax: 408-375-0501
Counties Served: Monterey
Case Restrictions: Must be a U.S. citizen or
legal resident.
Organization Email: itdept@crla.org

Nevada

Nevada County Lawyer Referral Service
Primary Address: 714 W Main St., 9th Floor
City: Nevada City
State: CA
Zip code: 95959
General Phone: 530-265-4129
Fax: 530-265-4139
Counties Served: Nevada
Case Types: Adoption, Bankruptcy,
Consumer, Child Custody, Dissolution of
Marriage, Elder Law, Employment, Real
Estate, Torts, Wills

Orange

Public Law Center
Primary Address: 601 Civic Center Drive
West
City: Santa Ana
State: CA
Zip code: 92701-4002
General Phone: 714-541-1010
Fax: 714-541-5157
Counties Served: Orange
Case Types: Adoption, Bankruptcy,
Community Economic Development,
Consumer, Child Custody, Dissolution of
Marriage, Domestic Violence, Elder Law,
Housing, Immigration, Real Estate, Torts,
Wills
Case Restrictions: Clients must meet
California IOLTA program income eligibility
requirements (75% of HUD 'low income'
figure for county).
Web Site: http://www.publiclawcenter.org

Placer

Legal Services of Northern California Mother
Lode Office-VLSP
Primary Address: 190 Reamer St.
City: Auburn

State: CA
Zip code: 95603-4721
General Phone: 530-823-7560
Fax: 530-823-7601
Counties Served: Amador, Calaveras, El
Dorado, Nevada, Placer, Sierra
Case Types: AIDS/HIV, Consumer, Child
Custody, Dissolution of Marriage, Elder Law,
Housing, Individual Rights, Public Benefits,
Wills
Other Case Types: Health

Riverside

Desert AIDS Project Legal Services
Primary Address: 750 South Vella Road
City: Palm Spring
State: CA
Zip code: 92264
General Phone: 619-323-2118
Fax: 619-323-9865
Case Types: AIDS/HIV

Inland Empire Latino Lawyers Association, Inc.
Primary Address: 2060 University Ave., Suite
113
City: Riverside
State: CA
Zip code: 92507-5210
General Phone: 951-369-3009
Fax: 951-369-6211
Intake Phone: 951-369-3009
Counties Served: Riverside, San Bernardino
Case Types: Consumer, Child Custody,
Dissolution of Marriage, Domestic Violence,
Housing, Individual Rights, Termination of
Parental Rights, Torts
Other Case Types: Educate teen parents and
pregnant minors on issues re: custody/visita-
tion, child support, establish paternity, TRO.
Case Restrictions: Program utilizes the LSC
Income Eligibility Guidelines set at 125% of
poverty, up to a maximum of 150% of the
guidelines. IELLA provides service to legal
and non-legal residents.
Web Site: http://www.iellaaid.org
Organization Email: iellaaid@aol.com

Riverside County Bar Association Public
Service Law Corp.
Primary Address: 4129 Main St., Suite 101
City: Riverside
State: CA
Zip code: 92501-3628

General Phone: 909-682-5213 (Admin.)
Fax: 909-682-0106
Intake Phone: 909-682-7968
Counties Served: Riverside
Case Types: Adoption, Consumer, Child
Custody, Dissolution of Marriage, Domestic
Violence, Housing, Real Estate, Torts, Wills
Other Case Types: Guardianships

Sacramento

Voluntary Legal Services Program of Northern
California, Inc.
Primary Address: 517 12th Street
City: Sacramento
State: CA   Zip code: 95814-1418
General Phone: 916-551-2116
Fax: 916-551-2120
Intake Phone: 916-551-2102
Counties Served: El Dorado, Placer,
Sacramento, San Joaquin, Yolo
Case Types: Bankruptcy, Consumer, Housing,
Public Benefits, Torts
Other Case Types: Conservatorships, Criminal
Records Expungement, Debt Collection
Defense, Estate Planning, Guardianships,
Landlord/Tenant, Probate
Case Restrictions: All LSC restrictions
Web Site: http://www.vlsp.org

Women Escaping A Violent Environment -
WEAVE
Primary Address: 1900 K St.
City: Sacramento
State: CA
Zip code: 95814-4107
General Phone: 916-448-2321
Fax: 916-448-0270
Intake Phone: 916-448-2321
Counties Served: Sacramento
Case Types: Domestic Violence
Case Restrictions: Must be a victim of domes-
tic violence.

San Bernardino

Legal Aid Clinic of Redlands
Primary Address: 16 E Olive Ave.
City: Redlands
State: CA
Zip code: 92373-5248
General Phone: 909-792-2762
Fax: 909-793-8788
Counties Served: San Bernardino

Case Types: Bankruptcy, Child Custody, Dissolution of Marriage, Domestic Violence, Elder Law, Termination of Parental Rights
Case Restrictions: Must be a resident of San Bernardino.

Legal Aid Society of San Bernardino, Inc.
Primary Address: 354 W Sixth St.
City: San Bernardino
State: CA
Zip code: 92401-1201
General Phone: 909-889-7328
Fax: 909-889-6338
Counties Served: San Bernardino
Case Types: Child Custody, Dissolution of Marriage, Domestic Violence, Housing
Case Restrictions: LSC restrictions

San Diego
Center for Community Solutions Domestic Violence Legal Clinic
Primary Address: 4508 Mission Bay Dr.
City: San Diego
State: CA
Zip code: 92109-4919
General Phone: 619-272-5328
Fax: 619-272-5361
Counties Served: San Diego
Case Types: Child Custody, Dissolution of Marriage, Domestic Violence
Case Restrictions: Must pertain to domestic violence.
Organization Email: info@ccssd.org

Elder Law & Advocacy Senior Citizens Legal Services
Primary Address: 3675 Ruffin Road 315
City: San Diego
State: CA
Zip code: 92123
General Phone: 858-565-1392
Fax: 858-565-1394
Intake Phone: 858-565-1392
Counties Served: Imperial, San Diego
Case Types: Elder Law
Other Case Types: General Civil, Elder Abuse, Nursing Home.
Case Restrictions: No criminal matters.
Web Site: http://seniorlaw-sd.org

San Diego Volunteer Lawyer Program
Primary Address: 625 Broadway, Suite 925
City: San Diego

State: CA
Zip code: 92101-5499
General Phone: 619-235-5656
Fax: 619-235-5668
Intake Phone: 619-235-5656
Counties Served: San Diego
Case Types: Child Custody, Dissolution of Marriage, Domestic Violence, Education, Elder Law, Health, Immigration, Individual Rights, Wills
Other Case Types: Family Law Mediation, Guardianship.
Case Restrictions: Applicant must be financially eligible for assistance.
Web Site: http://www.sdvlp.org

San Diego Volunteer Lawyer Program AIDS Law Team
Primary Address: 625 Broadway, Suite 925
City: San Diego
State: CA
Zip code: 92101-5499
General Phone: 619-235-5656 ext. 105
Fax: 619-235-5668
Counties Served: San Diego
Case Types: Bankruptcy, Dissolution of Marriage, Domestic Violence, Housing, Individual Rights, Public Benefits, Wills
Other Case Types: HIV/AIDS issues
Case Restrictions: Clients have to prove by medical records that they are HIV positive.
Web Site: http://www.sdvlp.org

San Francisco
AIDS Legal Referral Panel of the San Francisco Bay Area
Primary Address: 582 Market St.
City: San Francisco
State: CA
Zip code: 94104-5310
General Phone: 415-291-5454
Fax: 415-291-5833
Case Types: AIDS/HIV, Adoption, Bankruptcy, Consumer, Child Custody, Dissolution of Marriage, Employment, Health, Housing, Individual Rights, Public Benefits, Real Estate, Termination of Parental Rights, Torts, Wills
Case Restrictions: HIV+ or HIV related legal issue.
Web Site: http://www.alrp.org/

API Legal Outreach
Primary Address: 1188 Franklin St., Suite 202
City: San Francisco
State: CA
Zip code: 94109-6852
General Phone: 415-567-6255
Fax: 415-567-6248
Counties Served: Alameda, San Francisco, San Mateo
Case Types: Consumer, Child Custody, Dissolution of Marriage, Domestic Violence, Individual Rights, Public Benefits, Wills
Other Case Types: Elder Abuse

Cooperative Restraining Order Clinic
Primary Address: 3543 - 18th Street, 3rd Floor, Box #5
City: San Francisco
State: CA
Zip code: 94110
General Phone: 415-864-1790
Fax: 415-241-9491
Intake Phone: 415-252-2844
Counties Served: San Francisco
Case Types: Domestic Violence
Organization Email: roclinic@aol.com

Lawyers' Committee For Civil Rights Legal Services For Entrepreneurs
Primary Address: 131 Steuart Street 400
City: San Francisco
State: CA
Zip code: 94117
General Phone: 415-543-9444
Fax: 415-543-0296
Intake Phone: 415-543-9444
Counties Served: Alameda, Contra Costa, San Francisco
Case Types: Community Economic Development
Other Case Types: Legal Services for Entrepreneurs provides free business legal services to: low-income individuals, including women and persons of color, who want to start or develop businesses.
Case Restrictions: Eligibility Guidelines when reviewing an application for services, LSE will consider both the individual and his/her business's impact on the surrounding community. LSE will provide services to higher income applicants only under certain circumstances.
Web Site: http://www.lccr.com
Organization Email: helen@lcc.r.com

Lawyers' Committee Civil Rights of the San Francisco Bay Area
Primary Address: 301 Mission St., Suite 400
City: San Francisco
State: CA
Zip code: 94105-2258
General Phone: 415-543-9444
Fax: 415-543-0296
Counties Served: San Francisco
Case Types: Community Economic Development, Consumer, Education, Housing, Individual Rights
Other Case Types: Asylum
Case Restrictions: Must be low-income.

Legal Services for Children
Primary Address: 1254 Market St., 3rd Floor
City: San Francisco
State: CA
Zip code: 94102-4801
General Phone: 415-863-3762
Fax: 415-863-7708
Intake Phone: 415-863-3762
Counties Served: Alameda, Contra Costa, Marin, Napa, San Francisco, San Mateo, Santa Clara, Solano, Sonoma
Case Types: AIDS/HIV, Education, Juvenile
Other Case Types: Guardianship
Case Restrictions: Our office only represents minors.

ORAM International (Organization For Refuge Asylum & Migration)
Primary Address: 39 Drumm Street
City: San Francisco
State: CA Zip code: 94111
General Phone: (415) 399-1701
Fax: (415) 371-9191
Counties Served: National, International Other Case Types: Asylum, Immigration
Case Restrictions: ORAM is currently providing representation and assistance to lesbians, gays, bisexual, transgender, and intersex (LGBTI) refugees and asylum seekers. We serve our clients without regard to race, religion, nationality, ethnicity, gender, age or political persuasion. We work to assure the safety and security of all persons who fall within our mission.
Web Site: http://www.oraminternational.org
Organization Email: info@oraminternational.org

Volunteer Legal Services Program of The Bar Association of San Francisco
Primary Address: 301 Battery Street, 3rd Floor
City: San Francisco
State: CA
Zip code: 94111
General Phone: 415-982-1600
Fax: 415-477-2390
Intake Phone: 415-989-1616
Counties Served: Alameda, Contra Costa, Marin, San Francisco, San Mateo, Santa Clara
Case Types: Adoption, Bankruptcy, Community Economic Development, Consumer, Child Custody, Dissolution of Marriage, Domestic Violence, Elder Law, Health, Housing, Immigration, Individual Rights, Public Benefits, Torts, Wills
Other Case Types: Homelessness, SSI issues
Case Restrictions: Financial eligibility largely based on state definition of low income but varies by project; ability to work with volunteers.
Web Site: http://www.sfbar.org/jdc/index.aspx

Workers' Rights Clinic Employment Law Center
Primary Address: 1663 Mission St., Suite 400
City: San Francisco
State: CA
Zip code: 94103-2449
General Phone: 415-864-8848
Fax: 415-864-8199
Intake Phone: 415-864-8208
Counties Served: Alameda, Contra Costa, San Mateo, Marin, Santa Clara, Sonoma, San Francisco
Case Types: Employment
Web Site: http://employmentlawcenter.org

San Joaquin

Community Services AIDS Program
Primary Address: 1601 East Hazelton Avenue
City: Stockton
State: CA
Zip code: 95201-2009
General Phone: 209-468-2235
Fax: 209-468-3495
Case Types: AIDS/HIV

San Luis Obispo

San Luis Obispo Legal Alternatives Corporation
Primary Address: 1160 Marsh St., Suite 114
City: San Luis Obispo
State: CA
Zip code: 93401-3377
General Phone: 805-544-7997 (Admin.)
Fax: 805-544-3904
Intake Phone: 805-544-7995
Counties Served: San Luis Obispo
Case Types: Adoption, Bankruptcy, Consumer, Domestic Violence, Elder Law, Housing, Public Benefits, Real Estate, Torts, Wills

San Mateo

Legal Aid Society Of San Mateo County
Primary Address: 521 East 5th Ave.
City: San Mateo
State: CA
Zip code: 94402
General Phone: 650-558-0915
Fax: 650-558-0673
Intake Phone: 650-558-0915
Counties Served: San Mateo Case Types: Consumer, Education, Elder Law, Health, Housing
OtherCase Types: Assistance for Seniors, Conservatorships, Guardianships, Special Education and General Civil Litigation Referral
Case Restrictions: Low-Income
Web Site: http://www.legalaidsmc.org

Stanford Community Law Clinic
Primary Address: 2117 University Avenue, Suite A
City: East Palo Alto
State: CA
Zip code: 94303
General Phone: 650-475-0560
Fax: 650-326-4162
Counties Served: San Mateo, Santa Clara
Case Types: Employment, Housing
Case Restrictions: LSC guidelines
Web Site: http://www.freelegalaid.com/nav/california/other/resource/stanford-community-law-clinic

San Rafael

Legal Aid of North Bay Private Attorney Involvement Program
Primary Address: 1227 Coombs St.
City: Napa
State: CA
Zip code: 94559-2539
General Phone: 707-255-4933
Fax: 707-255-2312

Intake Phone: 800-498-7666
Counties Served: Napa, Marin
Case Types: AIDS/HIV, Adoption,
Bankruptcy, Community Economic
Development, Consumer, Child Custody,
Dissolution of Marriage, Domestic Violence,
Education, Elder Law, Employment, Health,
Housing, Immigration, Individual Rights,
Juvenile, Public Benefits, Real Estate,
Termination of Parental Rights, Torts, Wills
Case Restrictions: Residence in Marin or
Napa counties.
Organization Email: justice@legal-aid.marin.
ca.us

Santa Clara

AIDS Legal Services
Primary Address: 111 W Saint John St., Suite
315
City: San Jose
State: CA
Zip code: 95113-1104
General Phone: 408-293-3135
Fax: 408-293-0106
Counties Served: Santa Clara
Case Types: AIDS/HIV, Bankruptcy,
Consumer, Child Custody, Dissolution of
Marriage, Housing, Individual Rights, Public
Benefits, Real Estate, Torts, Wills
Case Restrictions: Must be HIV/AIDS positive.
Next Door Solutions to Domestic Violence
Legal Advocacy Program
Primary Address: 1181 N 4th St.
City: San Jose
State: CA
Zip code: 95112-4945
General Phone: 408-279-7550
Fax: 408-279-7562
Intake Phone: 408-279-7550
Counties Served: Santa Clara
Case Types: Domestic Violence
Case Restrictions: Client must be a victim of
domestic violence.

Pro Bono Project of Silicon Valley
Primary Address: 480 N 1st St., Suite 219
City: San Jose
State: CA
Zip code: 95112-4040
General Phone: 408-998-5298
Fax: 408-971-9672
Intake Phone: 408-998-5298
Counties Served: Santa Clara

Case Types: Adoption, Bankruptcy,
Consumer, Child Custody, Dissolution of
Marriage, Domestic Violence, Education,
Elder Law, Employment, Health, Housing,
Immigration, Individual Rights, Juvenile, Real
Estate, Torts

Public Interest Law Firm
Primary Address: 111 W Saint John St., Suite
315
City: San Jose
State: CA
Zip code: 95113-1104
General Phone: 408-293-4790
Fax: 408-293-0106
Counties Served: Santa Clara
Case Types: AIDS/HIV, Consumer,
Education, Elder Law, Employment, Health,
Housing, Immigration, Individual Rights,
Juvenile, Public Benefits, Torts
Case Restrictions: No class action and/or
impact litigation

Santa Cruz

California Rural Legal Assistance
Primary Address: 21 Carr St.
City: Watsonville
State: CA
Zip code: 95076-4705
General Phone: 831-724-2253
Fax: 831-724-7530
Counties Served: Monterey, Santa Cruz
Case Types: Bankruptcy, Domestic Violence,
Education, Housing, Public Benefits
Web Site: http://www.crla.org
Organization Email: itdept@crla.org

Solano

Legal Services of Northern California Solano
County Office
Primary Address: 1810 Capitol St.
City: Vallejo
State: CA
Zip code: 94590-5721
General Phone: 707-643-0054
Fax: 707-643-0144
Intake Phone: 707-643-0054
Counties Served: Solano
Case Types: Community Economic
Development, Consumer, Dissolution of
Marriage, Domestic Violence, Education,
Elder Law, Employment, Health, Housing,
Individual Rights, Public Benefits

Case Restrictions: We follow legal services corporation client eligibility guidelines and restrictions.
Web Site: http://lsnc.net

Sonoma

Sonoma County Legal Aid
Primary Address: 37 Old Courthouse Sq. 100
City: Santa Rosa
State: CA
Zip code: 95404-4033
General Phone: 707-542-1290
Fax: 707-542-1195
Intake Phone: 707-542-1290
Counties Served: Sonoma
Case Types: Consumer, Child Custody, Dissolution of Marriage, Domestic Violence, Housing
Other Case Types: Criminal Record Expungement
Case Restrictions: Various programs have certain restrictions. Our Self Help Access Center sees only low-income clients at poverty level or below. Our Legal Services Referral Project sees only welfare to work clients. We do information and referral for everyone.
Organization Email: sclapt@sonic.net

Sonoma County Legal Services Foundation
Primary Address: 1212 4th St., 1st Floor
City: Santa Rosa
State: CA
Zip code: 95404-4039
General Phone: 707-546-2924
Fax: 707-546-0263
Intake Phone: 707-546-2924
Counties Served: Sonoma
Case Types: Bankruptcy, Consumer, Child Custody, Domestic Violence, Employment, Housing, Juvenile, Wills

Stanislaus

California Rural Legal Assistance
Primary Address: 801 15th St., Suite11
City: Modesto
State: CA
Zip code: 95354-1132
General Phone: 209-577-3811
Fax: 209-577-1098
Case Types: Education, Elder Law, Employment, Housing, Individual Rights, Public Benefits
Case Restrictions: LSC restrictions

Web Site: http://www.crla.org

Haven Women's Center
Primary Address: 619 13th St., 1st Floor
City: Modesto
State: CA
Zip code: 95354-2435
General Phone: 209-524-4331
Fax: 209-424-2045
Counties Served: Stanislaus
Case Types: Child Custody, Domestic Violence
Case Restrictions: Client must be a victim of domestic violence or sexual assault and seeking protection from her perpetrator.

Ventura

AIDS Care Legal Clinic
Primary Address: 632 E Thompson Blvd.
City: Ventura
State: CA
Zip code: 93001
General Phone: 805-643-0446
Fax: 805-643-9474
Intake Phone: 805-643-0446
Counties Served: Ventura
Case Types: AIDS/HIV, Bankruptcy, Consumer, Individual Rights, Wills
Case Restrictions: Must either be a client or the family member of one of the agency's clients.

Conejo Free Clinic Legal Services
Primary Address: 80 E Hillcrest Dr., Suite 211
City: Thousand Oaks
State: CA
Zip code: 91360-7881
General Phone: 805-497-3575
Fax: 805-497-4099
Counties Served: Ventura
Case Types: Adoption, Bankruptcy, Consumer, Child Custody, Dissolution of Marriage, Domestic Violence, Elder Law, Employment, Health, Housing, Immigration, Individual Rights, Juvenile, Real Estate, Termination of Parental Rights

Grey Law of Ventura County
Primary Address: 290 Maple Ct., Suite 128
City: Ventura
State: CA
Zip code: 93003-3521
General Phone: 805-658-2266
Fax: 805-658-6339
Counties Served: Ventura

Case Types: Elder Law
Case Restrictions: 60+ years of age and
Ventura County resident

Ventura County Bar Association Volunteer
Legal Service Program
Primary Address: 4475 Market St., Suite B
City: Ventura
State: CA
Zip code: 93003-8051
General Phone: 805-650-7599
Fax: 805-650-8059
Intake Phone: 805-650-7599
Counties Served: Ventura
Case Types: Consumer, Child Custody,
Dissolution of Marriage, Domestic Violence,
Housing
Case Restrictions: Federal poverty guidelines.
Web Site: http://www.vcba.org
Organization Email: bar@vcba.org

Visalia

Central California Legal Services
Primary Address: 208 W Main St., U-1
City: Visalia
State: CA
Zip code: 93291
General Phone: 559-733-8770
Fax: 559-635-8096
Counties Served: Kings, Tulare
Case Types: Bankruptcy
Other Case Types: Family Law
Case Restrictions: We are restricted to serving
only those who qualify for services under LSC
guidelines. They must be low income and

a citizen of the U.S. or a lawful permanent
resident.
Web Site: http://www.centralcallegal.org
Organization Email: visalia@centralcallegal.org

Yolo

Legal Services of Northern California
Primary Address: 619 North St.
City: Woodland
State: CA
Zip code: 95695-3237
General Phone: 530-662-1065
Fax: 530-662-7941
Counties Served: Yolo
Case Types: Child Custody, Dissolution of
Marriage

Yuba

California Rural Legal Assistance
Primary Address: 818 D St.
City: Marysville
State: CA
Zip code: 95901-5321
General Phone: 530-742-5191 x310
Fax: 530-742-0421 Intake Phone: 530-742-
5191
Counties Served: Colusa, Sutter, Yuba
Case Types: Community Economic
Development, Education, Employment, Health,
Housing, Individual Rights, Public Benefits
Organization Email: itdept@crla.org

I realize that is a lengthy list and that's exactly the point. Free
Money options exist. This is just for the state of California. Go
research your state and I bet you will be amazed at what you discover. Free legal services abound!

Law Students

If you need help with your will or a divorce or bankruptcy or any kind of legal activity that has you a little perplexed, check out the free and reduced fee legal services in your community.

Did you know that many law schools have pro bono programs? Law students and their professors eat up pro bono work. They love it. They want to help people at the grass roots level. And we, the people, want to be helped without paying an arm and a leg.

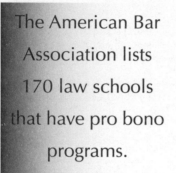
The American Bar Association lists 170 law schools that have pro bono programs.

The American Bar Association lists 170 law schools that have pro bono programs. How would you like a Harvard lawyer on your case? Or at least a Harvard law student? Maybe Columbia University School of Law? The most prestigious law schools in the country offer free and reduced fee legal services.

To see the complete list of law schools that offer public service and pro bono work, visit:

http://apps.americanbar.org/legalservices/probono/lawschools/pb_programs_chart.html.

Many of these schools require students to perform public service as a graduation requirement. For all kinds of pro bono information and resources visit: http://www.americanbar.org/groups/probono_public_service.html.

Foreclosure Aid

As we all know, foreclosures were once a random occurrence. Now, sadly, they're all too common. Because of the onslaught of foreclosure nightmares, more people than ever need legal help in this area.

If you're among those with housing issues, there is help available. The Institute for Foreclosure Legal Assistance exists to provide help to Americans losing their homes. Your state probably has an office.

Look up www.foreclosurelegalassistance.org/index.php. Here is a sample listing:

California
Legal Aid Foundation of Los Angeles
Housing and Economic Rights Advocates

Colorado
Colorado Legal Services

District of Columbia
Legal Counsel for the Elderly

Florida
Jacksonville Area Legal Aid
Legal Services of Greater Miami

Georgia
Atlanta Legal Aid Society

Illinois Legal Assistance Foundation of Metropolitan Chicago

Indiana
Indiana Legal Services Inc.

Iowa
Iowa Legal Aid

Kentucky
Appalachian Research and Defense Fund of Kentucky, Inc.

Louisiana
Southeastern Louisiana Legal Services

Maine
Pine Tree Legal Assistance

Maryland
Legal Aid Bureau of Maryland

Massachusetts
Neighborhood Legal Services, Inc.

Michigan
Legal Services of South Central Michigan

Minnesota
Mid-Minnesota Legal Services

Mississippi
Mississippi Legal Services

Missouri
Legal Services of Eastern Missouri, Inc.

Nevada
Legal Aid Center of Southern Nevada, Inc.

New York
Empire Justice Center
Staten Island Legal Services - Homeowner Defense Project
South Brooklyn Legal Services

North Carolina
Financial Protection Law Center
North Carolina Center for Justice

Ohio
Legal Aid Society of Cleveland
Legal Aid Society of Greater Cincinnati

Oregon
Oregon Law Center

Pennsylvania
Community Legal Services of Philadelphia

Texas
Texas Rio Grande Legal Aid

West Virginia
Mountain State Justice

Washington
Columbia Legal Services

Wisconsin
Legal Aid Society of Milwaukee

When you visit www.foreclosurelegalassistance.org/index.php, click on any of the legal service offices listed and you will be linked directly to their sites.

Maybe you personally are not facing foreclosure, but your landlord is. Renters are affected by this crisis, too. Many people are facing eviction, even though they pay their rent, because the landlord is dealing with foreclosure proceedings. If you are in this situation, legal aid is available to you as well.

The Institute for Foreclosure Legal Assistance exists to provide help to Americans losing their homes.

Hope for Homeowners

There are several services offering foreclosure help. The Homeownership Preservation Foundation has a national hotline dedicated to helping individuals facing foreclosure. You can call 888-995-HOPE.

The Homeownership Preservation Foundation has a single mission: to help homeowners avoid foreclosure. They are an independent nonprofit that provides HUD-approved counselors dedicated to helping homeowners. The help they offer is free.

Their counselors are experts in foreclosure prevention and trained to set up a plan of action designed just for you and your situation. When you talk to them, you won't be judged and you won't pay a dime. That's because they don't just offer general advice… they help you take action.

Their counselors will arm you with education and support that assists you in overcoming immediate financial issues… at no cost to you.

If you are facing foreclosure, give hope a chance. Visit www.995hope. org.

The American Bar Association also has foreclosure resources. Foreclosure tax tips can be found at:

http://www.americanbar.org/content/dam/aba/migrated/tax/ taxtips4u/ForeclosureTaxTips1.authcheckdam.pdf.

State laws regulate foreclosures, but there are national organizations that offer assistance, advice and guidance:

✔ AARP.org Foreclosure Information: www.aarp.org/money/ consumer

✔ Foreclosure Resources: http://www.usa.gov/Citizen/Topics/Family/Homeowners/Foreclosure.shtml

✔ Federal Trade Commission—Mortgage Info: http://www.consumer.ftc.gov/articles/0187-when-paying-mortgage-struggle

✔ HUD—Find a Housing Counselor: http://portal.hud.gov/hudportal/HUD?src=/i_want_to/talk_to_a_housing_counselor

✔ HUD—General Foreclosure Information: http://portal.hud.gov/hudportal/HUD?src=/topics/avoiding_foreclosure/fctimelineforeclosure

✔ HUD—Help for Homeowners Facing the Loss of Their Home: http://portal.hud.gov/hudportal/HUD?src=/homeownerhelp

✔ HUD—U.S. Department of Housing and Urban Development: www.hud.gov

✔ Housing Policy—Foreclosure prevention: http://www.housingpolicy.org/toolbox/foreclosure_landing.html

✔ Institute for Foreclosure Legal Assistance: www.foreclosurelegalassistance.org/resources

✔ LRI Foreclosure Materials: lri.lsc.gov/practice/foreclosure_resources.asp

✔ Legal Services National Technology Assistance Project: lsntap.org/foreclosure_efforts

✔ NeighborWorks America—Center for Foreclosure Solutions: www.nw.org/network/neighborworksprogs/foreclosuresolutions/default.asp

✔ Pine Tree Legal Services—Foreclosure Prevention Toolkit: http://www.ptla.org/foreclosure-prevention-toolkit

✔ Self-Help.org Subprime Response: http://www.self-help.org/about-us/community-impact/policy-initiatives.html

(Thanks to source ABA: http://apps.americanbar.org/legalservices/findlegalhelp/foreclosuremain.cfm)

To search for local legal resources in your state to help you with foreclosure or other matters, use:

http://apps.americanbar.org/legalservices/findlegalhelp/home.cfm

Free Advice

One more free resource you need to know (free resources = Free Money) is www.freeadvice.com. For legal advice, give a click and then narrow it down by your topic:

Accidents, Bankruptcy, Business, Criminal, Employment, Government, Injuries and Damages, Insurance, Intellectual Property, Litigation, Real Estate, Wills, Trusts, and Probate or General Practice.

FreeAdvice.com is not just for legal advice. They have more than 600,000 topics in their law section. They even cover insurance topics.

If you need a place to start, with any problem, free advice is always a good thing.

When you're playing on the Internet, feel free to check out any site that looks interesting. Read the information and the stories.

Free money stories are every- where. Here's a short list of some of our favorites:

- ✔ foundmoney.com
- ✔ unclaimedpropertydatabase.org/
- ✔ freemoney.com
- ✔ makefreecash.org
- ✔ freemoneysource.com
- ✔ mydollarplan.com
- ✔ cashunclaimed.com
- ✔ shop4freebies.com
- ✔ sweetfreestuff.com
- ✔ scholarships.com
- ✔ free.ed.gov

The information can be helpful. I only caution that you NOT pay a membership or a huge fee to find Free Money sources. There are a lot of free sites. Don't fall for scams. If you're ever in doubt of a Free Money source, contact your state agency. When it comes to unclaimed assets, states are the caretakers anyway.

If you need a place to start, with any problem, free advice is always a good thing.

CHAPTER 20

Signing Off

*"The chance that you or someone you know has
unclaimed property is greater than you think.
Finding out is free and easy."*
~Alexi Giannoulias, Illinois State Treasurer

*"The chance that you or someone you know has Free Money
is greater than you think. Finding out is free and easy."*
~Kevin Trudeau

I hope it's 100% clear to you now that there is Free Money out there, from a variety of sources, and through simple efforts, you can claim what's yours.

Even if the economy were doing great, which it's not, there are still all these outlets for Free Money to be had. In good times, and in bad times, these Free Money sources are there. It's time to seek them out.

It doesn't matter how rich you are, if you have Free Money coming your way, you should take it. The reality is that most folks aren't rich. Times are tough and these Free Money sources are needed now more than ever.

Review this book from time to time, and sign up for the monthly newsletters, which come to you chock-full of information to keep you up to date with the latest sources and information. The government is always creating new programs and tweaking old ones. New jackpots come to fruition all the time.

There's a disclaimer that you need to keep in mind. Some of the exact details of the sources and programs may change over time, but the reality of Free Money is still there. An individual program may change names, offices, or go defunct... but the existence of Free Money is still alive and well.

> In good times, and in bad times, these free money sources are there.

Send in your success stories. It could be grand and dramatic, or it could be like this online post from Anthony W.: "I had missing money. It was a check for $200 from the City of Lansing, MI. I lived there a few years back. I sent in a claim letter to the Unclaimed Property division of The Dept. of Treasury. They required additional verification. I sent in the verification and I received the check last week."

The information in the book will be worth more than the cost of the book itself.

There are many comments online. Check them out for yourself. And remember... you can read those online stories all you want, and you can read this book a dozen times, but if you don't try, you will never know if there is Free Money out there with your name on it.

In the very beginning chapters of the book, I mentioned that the proof is in the pudding. I looked up the origin of that phrase. The "word detective" (www.word-detective.com) gave this definition: "The proof is in the pudding" is a popular figure of speech meaning "the quality, effectiveness or truth of something can only be judged by putting it into action or to its intended use."

Here's the origin:

The proof is in the pudding' is actually a mangled form of the original phrase, which was "the proof of the pudding is in the eating." A dish may have been made from a good recipe with fresh ingredients and looks delicious, but you can really only judge it by putting it in your mouth. The actual taste is the only true criterion of success."

The proof of the *Free Money* Free Money book is in the doing. You can judge it only by trying some of these methods and seeing what happens for you. I know these methods work. Thousands and millions of other people know these methods work. Deep down, you believe these methods work, too, or you wouldn't have bought the book.

The temptation of Free Money is certainly delicious, but you will only know the reality of its true goodness when it's in your hands. The actual result is the only true criterion of success.

Agreed?

The proof of the pudding is in the eating. The proof of the *Free Money* Free Money book is in the doing. Give it a try. The ingredients are all right here. It's time to eat the pudding.

To your Free Money success!

State Agencies— Unclaimed Property

Every state has an office that handles unclaimed assets. To help you quickly find your "lost loot," we completely revamped the agency list to include the most accurate, up-to-date listings with snail mail addresses, email addresses (if available), web sites with direct link URLs and phone numbers.

Since the first Free Money book was published, many of these offices changed their info. As we send this book off to the printer's hands, we have the most accurate information available.

You can go to one online source and click directly on a state. Go to: http://nupn.com/state.php

Thank you National Unclaimed Property Network!

Alabama
State Treasury, Unclaimed Property
Division
P.O. Box 302520
Montgomery, AL 36130-2520
Phone: 334-242-9614 / 888-844-8400
www.moneyquestalabama.com

Alaska
Department of Revenue, Treasury
Division, Unclaimed Property Program
P.O. Box 110405
Juneau, AK 99811-0405
Phone: 907-465-3726
Fax: 907-465-2394
http://treasury.dor.alaska.gov

Arizona
Department of Revenue, Unclaimed
Property Unit
P.O. Box 29026
Phoenix, AZ 85038-9026
Phone: 602-364-0380 / 877-492 -9957
Fax: 602-542-2089
unclaimedproperty@azdor.gov
www.azunclaimed.gov

Arkansas
Unclaimed Property Division, Auditor
of State
P.O. Box 251906
Little Rock, AR 72225-1906
Phone: 501-682-6030 / 800-252-4648
claimit@auditor.ar.gov
www.ark.org/auditor/unclprop/index.
php/search/searchCrit

California
State Controller, Unclaimed Property
Division
P.O. Box 942850
Sacramento, CA 94250-5873
Phone: 916-454-2636 / 800-992-4647
http://scoweb.sco.ca.gov/UCP/

or

State Controller, Unclaimed Property
Division
777 South Figueroa Street, Suite 4800
Los Angeles, California 90017
Phone: 213-833-6010 / 800-992-4647
http://scoweb.sco.ca.gov/UCP/

Colorado
Unclaimed Property Division
1580 Logan St., Suite 500
Denver, CO 80203
Phone: 303-866-6070
Fax: 303-866-6154
www.colorado.gov/apps/treasury/ucp/
claims/personalSearch.faces

Connecticut
Office of State Treasurer, Unclaimed
Property Unit
55 Elm Street
Hartford, CT 06106
Phone: 800-833-7318
www.ctbiglist.com

Delaware
Bureau of Unclaimed Property
P.O. Box 8931
Wilmington, DE 19899
Phone: 302-577-8220
escheat.claimquestions@state.de.us
www.revenue.delaware.gov/unprop/
unprop_search.shtml

District of Columbia
Office of Finance Treasury, Unclaimed
Property Office
Unit 810 First Street NE, Room 401
Washington, DC 20002
Phone: (202) 442-8181
DCUnclaimed.Property@dc.gov
http://cfo.washingtondc.gov/cfo/cwp/
view,a,1326,q,590719,.asp

Florida
Department of Financial Services,
Bureau of Unclaimed Property
P.O. Box 8599
Tallahassee, FL 32314-8599
Phone: 888-258-2253 / 850-413-5555
FloridaUnclaimedProperty@
MyFloridaCFO.com
www.fltreasurehunt.org

Georgia
Georgia Department of Revenue,
Unclaimed Property Program
4125 Welcome All Road
Atlanta, Georgia 30349
Phone: (855) 329-9863
Fax: 404-724-7013
ucpmail@dor.ga.gov
https://etax.dor.ga.gov/ptd/ucp/index.aspx

Hawaii
State of Hawaii, Unclaimed Property
Program
P.O. Box 150
Honolulu, HI 96810
Phone: 808-586-1589
www.ehawaii.gov/lilo/app

Idaho
State Treasurer, Unclaimed Property
P.O. Box 83720
Boise, ID 83720-9101
Phone: 877-388-2942 / 208-332-2942
Fax: 208-332-2970
http://sto.idaho.gov/UnclaimedProperty

Illinois
Office of State Treasurer, Unclaimed
Property Division
P.O. Box 19495
Springfield, IL 62794-9495
Phone: 217-785-6998
http://icash.illinois.gov

Indiana
Office of the Indiana Attorney General
Unclaimed Property Division
PO Box 2504
Greenwood, IN 46142
Phone: (866) IN-CLAIM
www.indianaunclaimed.com/apps/ag/
ucp/index.html

Iowa
State Treasurer, Great Iowa Treasure
Hunt
Lucas State Office Building
321 East 12th Street, 1st Floor
Des Moines, IA 50319
Phone: 515-281-5367
foundit@iowa.gov
www.greatiowatreasurehunt.com/
pages/404/ref

Kansas
State Treasurer, Unclaimed Property
900 SW Jackson, Suite 201
Topeka, KS 66612-1235
Phone: 785-296-4165 / 800-432-0386
www.kansascash.com/prodweb/main/
index.php

Kentucky
State Treasury, Unclaimed Property
1050 US Highway 127 South, Suite 100
Frankfort, KY 40601
Phone: 502-564-4722
Fax: 502-564-6545
https://secure.kentucky.gov/treasury/
unclaimedProperty/Default.aspx

Louisiana
State Treasurer, Unclaimed Property
Division
P.O. Box 91010
Baton Rouge, LA 70821-9010
Phone: 225-219-9400
https://www.treasury.state.la.us/ucpm/
UP/UP_Search.asp

Maine
State Treasurer's Office, Unclaimed
Property
39 State House Station
Augusta, ME 04333-0039
Phone: 207-624-7470 / 888-283-2808
www.maine.gov/treasurer/unclaimed_
property

Maryland
Unclaimed Property Unit
301 W. Preston Street
Baltimore, MD 21201-2385
Phone: 1-800-782-7383 / 410-767-1700
(Baltimore area)
https://interactive.marylandtaxes.com/
Individuals/Unclaim/default.aspx

Massachusetts
Department of the State Treasurer,
Unclaimed Property Division
1 Ashburton Place, 12th Floor
Boston, MA 02108-1608
Phone: 1-800-647-2300 / 617-367-0400
http://abpweb.tre.state.ma.us/abp/
frmNewSrch.aspx

Michigan
Department of Treasury, Unclaimed
Property Division
P.O. Box 30756
Lansing, MI 48909
Phone: 517-636-5320
Fax: 517-322-5986
www.michigan.gov/
treasury/0,1607,7-121-44435-7924--,00.
html

Minnesota
Minnesota Department of Commerce,
Unclaimed Property Division
85 7th Place East, Suite 500
St. Paul, MN 55101-3165
Phone: 651-296-2568/ 800-925-5668
(Minnesota)
Fax: 651-282-2568
unclaimed.property@state.mn.us
www.commerce.state.mn.us/DOC_
Unclaimed_Property_Lookup.htm

Mississippi
State Treasurer, Unclaimed Property
Division
P.O. Box 138
Jackson, MS 39205
Phone: 601-359-3600
Fax: 601-359-2001
www.treasury.state.ms.us/Unclaimed/

Missouri
State Treasurer's Office, Unclaimed
Property Section
P.O. Box 1004
Jefferson City, MO 65102
Phone: 573-751-0123
www.treasurer.mo.gov/content/find-
your-property

Montana
Department of Revenue, Unclaimed
Property Division
Sam W. Mitchell Bldg.
125 N. Roberts, 3rd Floor
Helena, MT 59604
Phone: 1-866-859-2254
Fax: 406-444-7997
http://revenue.mt.gov/forbusinesses/
unclaimed_property/default.mcpx

Nebraska
Unclaimed Property Division
809 P Street
Lincoln, NE 68508
Phone : 402-471-2455
www.treasurer.state.ne.us/up/
upsearchprop.asp

Nevada
Office of the State Treasurer, Unclaimed
Property Division
Grant Sawyer Building
555 E. Washington Avenue, Suite 4200
Las Vegas, NV 89101
Phone: 702-486-4140 / 800-521-0019
(Nevada)
Fax: (702) 486-4140
unclaimedproperty@nevadatreasurer.gov
https://nevadatreasurer.gov/
UnclaimedProperty_Forms.htm

New Hampshire
Treasury Department, Unclaimed
Property Division
25 Capitol Street, Room 121
Concord, NH 03301
Phone: 603-271-2621 / 800-791-0920
(New Hampshire)
Fax: 603-271-3922
ap@treasury.state.nh.
www.nh.gov/treasury/Divisions/AP/
APindex.htm

New Jersey
Department of the Treasury, Unclaimed
Property
P.O. Box 214
Trenton, NJ 08695-0214
Phone: 609-292-9200
Fax: 609-984-0593
www.unclaimedproperty.nj.gov

New Mexico
Taxation & Revenue Department,
Unclaimed Property Division
P.O. Box 630
Santa Fe, NM 87504
Phone: 505-827-0700
www.tax.newmexico.gov/Online-
Services/Pages/Unclaimed-Property-
Search.aspx

New York
State Comptroller, State Office of
Unclaimed Funds
110 State Street
Albany, NY 12236
Phone: 800-221-9311
NYSOUF@osc.state.ny.us
www.osc.state.ny.us/ouf/contacts.htm

North Carolina
Department of State Treasurer, Escheat
& Unclaimed Property
325 North Salisbury Street
Raleigh, NC 27603
Phone: 919-508-1000
unclaimed.property@nctreasurer.com
www.nctreasurer.com/Claim-Your-Cash/
Claim-Your-NC_Cash/Pages/default.aspx

North Dakota
State Land Department, Unclaimed
Property Division
1707 North 9th Street
P.O. Box 5523
Bismarck, ND 58506-5523
Phone 701-328-2800
Fax: 701-328-3650
www.land.nd.gov/UnclaimedProperty/
Individuals.aspx

Ohio
Department of Commerce, Division of
Unclaimed Funds
77 South High Street, 20th floor
Columbus, OH 43215-6108
Phone: 614-466-4433
Fax: 614-752-5078
unfd.claims@com.state.oh.us
www.com.ohio.gov/unfd/TreasureHunt.aspx

Oklahoma
Oklahoma State Treasurer's Office,
Unclaimed Property Division
2401 NW 23rd Street, Suite 42
Oklahoma City, OK 73107
Phone: 405-521-4273
unclaimed@treasurer.ok.gov
www.ok.gov/treasurer/Unclaimed_
Property/index.html

Oregon
Department of State Lands
Unclaimed Property Section
775 Summer Street NE Suite 100
Salem OR 97301-1279
Phone: 503-986-5289
Fax: 503-378-4844
claims@dsl.state.or.us
https://oregonup.us/upweb/up/up_login.
asp

Pennsylvania
Pennsylvania Treasury Department,
Unclaimed Property
129 Finance Building
Harrisburg, PA 17120
Phone: 800-222-2046
tupmail@patreasury.org
www.patreasury.gov/Unclaimed/Search.
html

Rhode Island
Treasury Office, Unclaimed Property
Manager
State House, Room 102
Providence, RI 02903
Telephone: 401-222-2397
Fax: 401-222-6140
generaltreasurer@treasury.ri.gov

www.treasury.ri.gov/divisions/
unclaimedproperty

South Carolina
State Treasurer's Office, Unclaimed
Property Program
P.O. Box 11778
Columbia, SC 29211
Phone: 803-737-4771
Fax: 803-734-2668
payback@sto.sc.gov
www.treasurer.sc.gov/palmetto_
payback_unclaimed_property/Pages/
SEARCHUNCLAIMEDPROPERTY.
aspx

South Dakota
Office of the State Treasurer
500 E. Capitol Ave.
Pierre, SD 57501-5070
Phone: 605-773-3379 / 866-357-2547
https://sdtreasurer.gov/
unclaimedproperty

Tennessee
Tennessee State Treasurer, Unclaimed
Property Division
502 Deaderick St.
Nashville, TN 37243-0203
Phone: 615-741-6499
ucp.information@tn.gov
https://apps.tn.gov/unclp

Texas
Texas Comptroller of Public Accounts,
Unclaimed Property Claims Section
P.O. Box 12046
Austin, TX 78711-2046
Phone: 1-800-654-3463 / 512-463-3120
(Austin)
Fax: 1-888-908-9991 / 512-936-6224
(Austin)
unclaimed.property@cpa.state.tx.us
www.window.state.tx.us/up

Utah
Treasurer's Office, Unclaimed Property
Division
168 N. 1950 W. Suite 102
Salt Lake City, UT 84116
Phone: 888-217-1203 / 801-715-3300
Fax: 801-715-3309
ucprop@utah.gov
www.mine.utah.gov/index.asp

Vermont
Vermont Unclaimed Property Division
State Treasurer's Office
109 State Street
Montpelier, Vermont 05609-6200
Phone: 802-828-2407 / 800-642-3191
treasurers.office@state.vt.us
www.vermonttreasurer.gov/unclaimed-
property

Virginia
Virginia Department of Treasury
101 North 14th Street
Richmond, VA 23219
Phone: 1-800-468-1088/ 804-225-2393
www.trs.virginia.gov/vaMoneySearch/
Account/LogOn

Washington
Department of Revenue, Unclaimed
Property Section
P.O. Box 47477
Olympia, WA 98504-7477
Phone: 800-435-2429 / 360-705-6706
http://ucp.dor.wa.gov/

West Virginia
West Virginia State Treasurer's Office,
Unclaimed Property Division
One Players Club Drive
Charleston, West Virginia 25311
Phone: 800-642-8687/ 304-558-2937
www.wvsto.com/dept/UP/Pages/default.
aspx

Wisconsin
Office of the State Treasurer Unclaimed
Property Unit
P.O. Box 2114
Madison, WI 53701-2114
Phone: 855-375-2274 / 608-267-7977
Fax: 608-261-6799
ostunclaimedproperty@wisconsin.gov
www.statetreasury.wisconsin.gov/section.
asp?linkid=1381&locid=155

Wyoming
Wyoming Unclaimed Property
2515 Warren Avenue, Suite 502
Cheyenne, WY 82002
Phone: 307-777-5590
http://treasurer.state.wy.us/uphome.asp

Canada

I realize we have some readers from Canada or who may have unclaimed assets there. Canada operates a little different from the United States. First of all, Canadian banks have a legal obligation to attempt written notification of account owners after the second and fifth year of inactivity.

I like that. Not sure why the two and five, but a legal obligation to contact owners of the assets is a good thing.

In the ninth year of inactivity, the Office of the Superintendent of Financial Institutions (OSFI) prepares a list of all unclaimed balances of $10 or more and the name of the owner. This list is published in the Canada Gazette, available at all public libraries. Year ten is when assets get transferred over to Bank of Canada.

O Canada

So Canada has a notice system in place. Very good.

Bank of Canada then becomes custodian when there has been no account activity for a ten-year period and the owner can't be contacted. Accounts worth $500 or more are held indefinitely until claimed. AND, get this, interest is paid at the rate of 1.5% per year for a ten-year period.

Balances under $500 are retained for twenty years—ten years from the date of the last owner transaction at the bank, with an additional ten-year custody period at Bank of Canada. To get the funds, a written claim must be received no later than December 31 of the account's "last year," which is twenty years after the year of the last transaction.

Make sense so far? If more than $500, it sits forever. If less than $500, you have twenty years to claim it.

Canada has millions of dollars of unclaimed money. More than two-thirds of it is sums that are less than $500.

The Bank of Canada has a database to search as well. To check it out and do a search, visit ucbswww.bank-banque-canada.ca. You can also contact it the old fashioned way:

> Dormant Account Section: Unclaimed Balances Services
> Bank of Canada
> 234 Wellington
> Ottawa, ON, K1A 0G9
> Phone: 800-303-1282
> Fax: 613-782-7713

For tax refunds, their version of the IRS is called Revenue Canada. They are holding an estimated $8 million in unclaimed tax refunds since 1990. There is no time limit on claims, but no interest is paid on amounts refunded. Privacy legislation prevents publication of owner names. Citizens should contact their local tax office for additional information.

Unclaimed asset practices with regard to items other than bank accounts and tax refunds vary by province.

If you are looking into assets for a deceased loved one, you must be able to prove a blood relation. Have date of death and other information available. For info on "how to prove you are an heir." For more information, visit:

www.attorneygeneral.jus.gov.on.ca/english/

In British Columbia, the Ministry of Finance and Corporate Relations administers the Unclaimed Property Office and maintains a searchable database. This database serves this province only. For more information, visit: www.bcunclaimedproperty.bc.ca

(Source: www.unclaimedassets.com/canada.htm)

United Kingdom

And for our friends across the pond, unclaimed property is very much the case there, too.

An old report from London's Financial Times stated, "There is a sea of unclaimed assets sloshing around the financial system." Back in 1999, the low estimate of unclaimed funds was £77 billion.

You know that number has to be A LOT more by now.

The funds are the same kind of thing that happens here in the States. Old bank accounts, unclaimed pensions, life insurance policies, securities, dividends, unredeemed national savings certificates and premium bonds.

One item I found interesting is that the United Kingdom unclaimed asset pool contains winnings from their national lottery. Wow. People win the lottery and don't claim it. See what I mean that money is sitting in unexpected places.

[Source: www.unclaimedassets.com/UK.htm]

Debt Statute of Limitations

This chart shows the length in years that each state has for its statute of limitations on various kinds of agreements. Most credit card debts are considered "open-ended accounts" and that means a very short statute period in many states. You could be passed the statute of limitations in just three years.

Check with your local advisor for any questions. As we go to press, this chart is accurate to the best of our knowledge.

State	Oral Contracts	Written Contracts	Promissory Notes	Open-ended Accounts
AL	6	6	6	3
AR	5	5	5	3
AK	6	6	3	3
AZ	3	6	6	3
CA	2	4	4	4
CO	6	6	6	3
CT	3	6	6	6
DE	3	3	3	4
DC	3	3	3	3
FL	4	5	5	4

State	Oral Contracts	Written Contracts	Promissory Notes	Open-ended Accounts
GA	4	6	6	4
HI	6	6	6	6
IA	5	10	5	5
ID	4	5	5	4
IL	5	10	10	5
IN	6	10	10	6
KS	3	5	5	3
KY	5	15	15	5
LA	10	10	10	3
ME	6	6	6	6
MD	3	3	6	3
MA	6	6	6	6
MI	6	6	6	6
MN	6	6	6	6
MS	3	3	3	3
MO	5	10	10	5
MT	3	8	8	5
NC	3	3	5	4
ND	6	6	6	6
NE	4	5	5	4
NH	3	3	6	3
NJ	6	6	6	6
NM	4	6	6	4
NV	4	6	3	4
NY	6	6	6	6
OH	6	15	15	6
OK	3	5	5	3
OR	6	6	6	6
PA	4	6	4	6
RI	10	10	6	4
SC	3	3	3	3
SD	6	6	6	6
TN	6	4	6	6
TX	4	4	4	4

State	Oral Contracts	Written Contracts	Promissory Notes	Open-ended Accounts
UT	4	6	6	4
VA	3	6	6	3
VT	6	6	5	4
WA	3	6	6	3
WI	6	6	10	6
WV	5	15	6	4
WY	8	10	10	8

[Source: poorcreditgenie.com/crstatutelim.html]